C000313447

Happiness is
a Ticked Off List!

`Inspection Copy only`

Karen Lindsey

Happiness is a Ticked Off List!

The comprehensive guide on how to organise
and manage a perfect corporate event

Copyright © 2009 Karen Lindsey

The moral right of the author has been asserted.

Apart from any fair dealing for the purposes of research or private study,
or criticism or review, as permitted under the Copyright, Designs and Patents
Act 1988, this publication may only be reproduced, stored or transmitted, in
any form or by any means, with the prior permission in writing of the
publishers, or in the case of reprographic reproduction in accordance with
the terms of licences issued by the Copyright Licensing Agency. Enquiries
concerning reproduction outside those terms should be sent to the publishers.

Matador
5 Weir Road
Kibworth Beauchamp
Leicester LE8 0LQ, UK
Tel: (+44) 116 279 2299
Fax: 0116 279 2277
Email: books@troubador.co.uk
Web: www.troubador.co.uk/matador

Legal Disclaimer
The author shall not be liable for any direct, indirect, special or consequential damages in contract, tort or otherwise,
arising out of the use of this book or the reliance of information in it. The contents of this paragraph shall apply to the
maximum extent permissible by applicable laws. Any rights not expressly granted herein are reserved. The author has
used reasonable care to ensure that the information in this book is accurate and up to date. Although the author has
taken precaution to prevent the occurrence of errors and omissions, the reader of this book should not take the
accuracy of the information for granted. None of the material in this book is to be relied upon as a statement or
representation of fact. English law and jurisdiction applies with respect to the contents of this book.
® All company and brand names used throughout this book are the registered trademarks of their respective companies.

BN 978 1848761 032

British Library Cataloguing in Publication Data.
A catalogue record for this book is available from the British Library.

Typeset in 11pt Bembo by Troubador Publishing Ltd, Leicester, UK
Printed in Great Britain by the MPG Books Group, Bodmin and King's Lynn

Matador is an imprint of Troubador Publishing Ltd

For Jeff Clogg
My tireless supporter. My inspiration. My father.

Contents

Introduction, Preface and Author's Biog   *ix*

The Step by Step Process   **1**

Chapter 1: Pre Production - Innovation   **3**

- Establishing the Brief   5
- Event Brief   7
- Location, Location, Location   9
- Administrative Housekeeping   17
- Guideline Costing   19
- Update Time   25
- Site Visit   25
- Costing Update   27
- Authorisation   28
- Confirmation   29

Chapter 2: Pre Production - Organisation   **33**

- The Itinerary   35
- The Benchmark Schedule   42

Chapter 3: Pre Production - Overall Event Design   **47**

- Theme   49
- Event Content and Suppliers   67

Chapter 4: Pre Production – Concluding Organisation   **75**

- Logistics   78
- Event Finalisation   88

Chapter 5: Production - On Site   **91**

- Banqueting Team Meeting   93
- Event Management Meeting   95
- Setting Up   96
- Ready to Go!   96
- What To Do When Things Don't go to Plan!   97
- Working in Advance   99

- Event Management   99
- End of Event   100
- Prior to Departure   101

Chapter 6: Post Production   **103**

- Final Costing   105
- Thank you   106
- File Management   106

Chapter 7: Health & Safety   **107**

- Event Organisers   109
- Suppliers   109
- Location   110
- On Site   111
- H&S Adviser   112
- A Word to the Wise   113

Chapter 8: Components and Considerations   **115**

- Conferences   117
- Award Ceremonies   126
- Team Building   128
- Activity Days   134
- Press and Product Launches   137
- Family Fun Days   141

Help is at Hand!   145

Chapter 9:   **Fifty Top Tip Ticks**   **147**

Chapter 10:   **The A-Z Survival Guide**   **157**

Chapter 11:   **Your Tool Box**   **167**

Chapter 12:   **The Ultimate Tick List**   **171**

Chapter 13:   **Complete Itinerary**   **193**

Chapter 14:   **Complete Benchmark Schedule**   **211**

Helpful Contact Details   **217**

Acknowledgements   **226**

General Index   **229**

Introduction

Having stumbled into event organising purely by accident, it never ceases to amaze me that, twenty one years on, I am still passionate about the job that I do.

I have organised hundreds of corporate events, with the majority of these having gone totally to plan but there have been a few (no matter how much precise planning applied) that simply took a very different course. So, the skill of a good event organiser isn't just about how to manage an event when it is going fantastically well, but it's also about how to cope when things don't go exactly to schedule. This book is my personal take on how best to organise an event and I will share with you how, with forethought and processes in place, it is my belief that even the most potentially disastrous situation can be turned into a true feat of perfection.

My motto is 'that will do, will NEVER do' and if you empathise with this sentiment then you are going to love this book. It will become your reference manual and trusted companion. However, for those of you who are not so great on attention to detail; let me allay your fears as this book will provide you with a tick list on how you can also achieve fantastic, consistent results with the least amount of fuss, stress and worry. As with my job, I am also passionate about sharing my experience with you and, at the end of this book, I hope that you will also feel passionate about your role as a proficient event organiser.

All emotions aside, when it comes to organising and managing events, although the job role sounds very exotic and exciting, really it is just damned hard work! Nevertheless, when you get it right (although there may be some tears along the way and most definitely some sore feet) the rewards are undeniably worth all the effort. I feel that it is one of only a handful of professions which allows you to see the job through from beginning to end and it is a role that I think I will still be doing for many years to come. It's in my blood.

Although it may or may not be in your blood, as budgets get tighter, more and more people are asked to organise events as part of their normal job specification. This book isn't just aimed at people who have to organise events on this basis. (You may already be a trainee in the industry or be an old hand but want a refresher. Or you may be an individual seeking a career change and would like a head start.) Whatever the circumstance, this book is for people who have to or want to perform and deliver with excellence but do not have the benefit of twenty one years event organisation knowledge to do so. Now, help is at hand – you can draw upon my many years of experience, quite literally at the turn of this page.

One thing that remains constant throughout, regardless, is the process that it takes in order to achieve the perfect event. This comprehensive guide will take you through a step by step process of event organising and, when the time comes, it will show you how to manage the event proficiently by utilising a very helpful tool, which I affectionately refer to as my 'event bible'. The end result being: happy guests or happy clients or perhaps a happy colleague or boss, but most importantly, happy you and by the time you have completed this book you will also fully appreciate why Happiness is truly a Ticked Off List!

Karen Lindsey

Preface

This step by step guide has been created solely to take you through the process on how to organise a successful event. I have not included any advice on setting up an event company, or the various legal requirements associated with running a corporate events business, nor have I provided comprehensive details on the various insurances and bureaucracy which have to be considered or indeed the procedure for issuing invoices and making/receiving various payments when working in this field.

I have, however, concentrated on providing guidance for those people who wish to organise events within the UK; working overseas (although sharing some of the same processes) is a different ball game altogether.

As this book has been written for a multitude of people who, in one way or another, are in the position to organise events, I have assumed that, whatever their circumstance, the persons in question are quite simply 'good to go'. If you would like any advice on the legalities pertaining to this industry or further clarification/assistance on any subject touched upon in this book, I have listed some addresses at the back of this publication (Helpful Contact Details) which you may find useful.

For the purpose of demonstrating the various processes, I have assumed that the person reading this book wishes to become a proficient event organiser and works in the capacity of organising events on behalf of his/her employers/company or has an end client. For either scenario, I have assumed that someone, whether this be a boss, colleague or client provides the original event brief, the 'brief provider'.

Author's Biog

Karen Lindsey is a respected professional with twenty one years experience of organising events for blue chip companies such as: KFC, Paramount Home Entertainment, Avis Europe, Coca Cola and Momentum Pictures, to name but a few.

Her career has been extremely varied – a trained and experienced secretary, model and subsequent model agent, she fell into event organising purely by accident. She found her forte and hasn't looked back since.

Having organised hundreds of successful corporate events, both within the UK and overseas, her notable projects have included: Project Manager for 'Race to Gotham City' to mark the release of the Batman video which culminated in a star studded party at Pinewood Studios, attended by the likes of Mel Gibson. Commissioned by UK Gold, she organised a celebrity football challenge, held at Wembley Stadium and captained by players of the 1966 England World cup team to mark the launch of Match of the Day on the channel. She produced themed parties, conferences and screenings for Universal Pictures based on films such as Shrek, Bridget Jones, Van Helsing, Thunderbirds and The Hulk and recently, she was logistical coordinator and event manager for the Mel B (of Spice Girls fame) Totally Fit UK Tour.

Karen has also received many accolades such as heading a Pilot Project for the British Army to make their facilities and staffing available to the corporate sector. She was instrumental in developing hospitality and sponsorship opportunities for the leading British Superbike Team, Rizla Suzuki and, after a gruelling twelve month selection process, was asked to become one of a handful of agencies awarded the position of 'preferred UK corporate event supplier' for Orange/France Telecom.

Karen ran her own events company for fourteen years and in 2005 she became an Event Consultant. 2009 saw the launch of her training wing – where she guest lectures at universities and hosts 'The Seminar', aimed at individuals who have a requirement to organise a corporate event. The seminar content, based on the information found in this book, is, too, a step by step guide on how to organise and manage a perfect corporate event.

The Step by Step Process

CHAPTER 1

Pre Production – Innovation

Pre Production – Innovation

No matter what type of event you are organising: a party, conference, awards ceremony, team building, activity day, press and product launch or family fun day, the only way that you can guarantee the event's success is PLANNING, PLANNING AND MORE PLANNING.

When events run smoothly, people tend to think that life as an event organiser is a simple one. However, events only normally appear to run effortlessly because of all the pre production planning that has been undertaken.

As the organiser, you are perceived and should strive to become, the smooth interface between the host of the event and all third party suppliers. It sounds like hard work but by following the simple steps that I am about to share with you, even the planning itself takes on a process which helps to identify exactly what it is you have to organise, the time scale in which it has to be achieved along with how to manage the duties within a set time frame, in small, manageable chunks.

I will ask you to don many a hat during the organisational process as, after all, you are Superman or Wonderwoman, aren't you? (Or so your boss, colleague or client may like to assume as you aspire to pulling even the biggest of rabbits out of the smallest of hats at just a moment's notice.) So, if you still want to embark on the 'I wish to be a proficient event organiser' journey, which provides little thanks but is of immense personal reward and are apt at displaying the serenity of a swan swimming on a calm lake whilst really paddling like crazy below water – event organising could certainly be for you.

My advice is to buy a very large hat stand, a snug computer chair and, for all you ladies out there, an array of attractive but remarkably comfy shoes.

Establishing the Brief

The first task on your *to do list* is to establish the brief. This may be with your boss, colleague or client – whoever it is for is immaterial, as the process is the same. This first stage of your pre production phase is where you start to ask some searching questions with a view to obtaining some considered answers. This 'identifying the brief' stage has to be undertaken for every event, whatever its nature. It will save you time and much energy in the end.

Top Tip Tick:

People often ask me what the ideal lead in time is for an event. I always give the same answer, as much time as possible. Unfortunately, you may not have a choice of when you are called in to take a brief but at least twelve weeks is a reasonable time frame. I prefer longer as you have more time to investigate, contemplate and action but I have had to turn around events within forty eight hours – I wouldn't recommend it, but it can be done. So try to obtain as much lead in time as possible. It is far less stressful for you and it makes for a better end result.

Although I will endeavour to provide guidance on the various steps throughout this book, my objective is to get you *thinking* like a proficient event organiser from the outset and so, just for a moment, let's get you in the right frame of mind.

Don your first hat, your 'guest' hat and grab yourself a pen and pad. Let's imagine you have personally been invited to a special occasion. As a guest, what do you immediately look for on the invite? Take a moment, prior to reading any further, to write down the key information you feel, as a recipient, you would like to know.

Done that? If you are like me, I immediately search for what the occasion is for and from whom? When is it? What time is it? Where is it? Is it just for me or can I take a guest? Applying your thought process to formulate a brief is just an extension of your thought process when receiving an invite.

Now, switch hats and don your 'event organiser' hat. Whilst considering the extended invitation scenario, as the event organiser, write down some key questions that you feel would need to be clarified from the brief provider.

Some of the key questions that I'd wish to be clarified would include:

- What is the event for?
- What type of event is required?
- Who is staging this event? (company/department)
- What is the preferred date?
- What are the timings?
- Where is the preferred location?
- Are partners invited?
- Who will be invited?
- What age group will be attending?
- What percentage of the guests are male and female?
- How many guests?

- What is the desired event format?
- Is food and drink required?
- Is entertainment required? (if relevant)
- What about a theme?
- Any decoration required? (if relevant)
- Any overnight accommodation required?
- What is the dress code?
- Is transportation to and from the location required?
- What is the key objective?
- Is this perceived as a 3★, 4★ or 5★ event?
- Have any events similar to this been arranged before?
  (If so: where, when and how successful were they?
  Anything in particular that worked well and anything that didn't?)
  and most importantly....
- What is the budget? (including or excluding VAT)

How did your questions compare? Once these types of questions have been posed, it will not only help the brief provider to re-consider all their objectives and to formulate an accurate requirement, it will help *you* when the answers have been fully considered. This is the starting point of your event organisation.

Top Tip Tick:

Don't be surprised when you have seemingly identified the event requirements and undertaken some initial research, the brief changes and you have to go back to the drawing board. Sometimes, considering the brief is only the start of the brief provider identifying exactly what they want. Take a deep breath and count to ten and try to factor into your planning that this situation may, indeed, arise.

Event Brief

Your next step would be to type yourself an Event Brief, which is a document that clarifies all the objectives of an event. This document, when kept close to hand, will help to constantly reaffirm the requirements of the event during the initial stages of the pre production period.

So now I have managed to get you thinking like a proficient event organiser, let's move this on to the next stage. To help explain and demonstrate a little better, from hereon in, I am going to work through the processes with you, based on a fictional event. For the purpose of this example, let's suppose that the brief provider is your boss. The following, in no particular order, are the answers to the questions posed previously overleaf:

Event Brief

Event:	Party To celebrate the opening of an office in Paris
Location:	Central London
Date:	July 24th
Guests:	200 guests/clients including partners. Twenty-fifty years of age 50/50 split male/female
Requirements:	Dinner, dancing and entertainment (Pre dinner drinks and wine with dinner)
Time:	19.30 – midnight
Theme:	French
Transportation:	None required
Budget:	Approx £140.00 plus VAT per head
Vision:	4★ event (but with 5★ service and style)
Note:	Accommodation only required for management team Dress code – formal Invitation required
Objective:	To celebrate this landmark and to thank the customers for their continued support. (Previous corporate events, although well attended, have not been particularly memorable as they followed a traditional format. This year, the format is to change with the emphasis being on fun with a break away from tradition.)

Top Tip Tick:

Once the Event Brief document has been typed, I find that it is a good idea to run this past the brief provider so an agreement can be obtained that his/her objectives have been completely understood, priorities identified and flexibility clarified. This should spur the person into clarifying his/her requirements prior to giving the authorisation to continue - saving valuable time, him/her money and most definitely your sanity.

Location, Location, Location

Consideration

So, now you have identified the event format and objectives, what's next?

One of the most important aspects of an event is the location selection. Apart from when organising a function within your company's or client's office building, no matter the type of event, you will need to find a suitable location.

The location not only has to be able to accommodate the function size but, most importantly, it has to be fitting to the image, demographics of the guests, event requirement and also to the theme, should there be one.

The golden rule is to study the Event Brief and contemplate whether there are any key aspects that need to be considered (depending upon the event in question). Later on in the book, I highlight some key considerations when choosing a location, taking into account each type of event - you may like to read these prior to undertaking a location search.

However, for the purpose of guiding you through this step by step process, let's assume that there are no particular aspects that need to be taken into account when considering the location – it just has to be fitting to the requirements of the fictional brief.

I suggest you always start by investigating two types of locations:

*   hotels
    or
*   venues

Top Tip Tick:

If an event has a specific theme, then in my opinion, this should be applied throughout all aspects of the function. This, therefore, begs the question; should the initial selection process of a location be because of its suitability to a theme or its adaptability potential?

It's a chicken and egg situation really as there is no correct answer to this dilemma. My solution is always to investigate locations thoroughly whilst keeping the event theme at the forefront of my mind.

As a rule of thumb, 'hotels' have accommodation and are normally specifically designed to host a range of events whilst 'venues' invariably do not have accommodation and offer facilities which have not been specifically designed for hosting functions but can be adapted to enable them to take place. Venues include establishments such as museums, stately homes or art galleries.

For instance, whilst considering the fictional brief… as the Party is a celebration to commemorate the opening of an office in Paris then there is an opportunity to create a specific theme, indeed, one has been requested. A location such as an art gallery housing Monet's paintings could potentially be a fitting venue but, when considering a fictional event of this nature, other factors also have to be contemplated, such as the availability of preparing the venue during opening hours and whether the location is conducive to high spirits.

The other consideration is whether the event is required to take place in an 'exclusive' environment. The chances are, if selecting an hotel, then the function may not be the only event taking place within the property. Consequently, if securing a venue, then some establishments will only run one event at any one time, which is great in one way but not so great on the pocket! Exclusive hire can be costly but if budget is no object, it is a fantastic way to ensure that the event is just that little bit more special.

A word of warning, however. If exclusively hiring a venue, such as a castle, then in addition to the hefty 'exclusivity' charge, you may also need to factor the costs for hiring in absolutely everything that is needed for the event such as tables, chairs, linen etc and when considering catering, the caterers will most probably need to hire all their catering equipment so costs can escalate.

It's really horses for courses. For this particular example, utilising a hotel which could be 'themed' to fit the occasion, provide the flexibility of overnight on site parking, the facility to set up and prepare during working hours, the ability to utilise party theming and to be able to dance plus the option of on–site accommodation – for me, that would probably tip the balance when considering a hotel rather than a venue. The fact that this fictional event does not have an unlimited budget would also be a key factor.

Search

If you have a knowledge of locations when considering a brief, normally one location in particular would spring to mind. Nonetheless, if you are a novice in this field, you may not know where to start.

There are two main options that you can take... if you are working within an event organisation or an individual acting on behalf of a client, then you most probably would like to undertake the location search yourself or, if you are working on behalf of a company which wishes to host the event, then you may like to call upon the services of a location/venue find agency.

To explain a little further... if you are a professional event organiser or a 'find' agency, most hotels and venues that wish to secure corporate business will pay the organiser or agent a 'placement' commission. This normally ranges between 8-10% of either anything 'pre booked★' or based on 'delegate' rates (net of VAT).

Unfortunately, commission is not paid by locations directly to the company hosting the event, so, if you are organising an event on behalf of a company that you work for, then I am afraid that agency commission cannot be secured. This means that, if wanting to cut out a lot of work, it may make sense to seek the services of a 'find' agency as you shouldn't be charged for a location find service because the agency would be paid commission by the location (although terms and conditions do apply and vary between each location find agency.)

Top Tip Tick:

The more information you can give a location/venue find agency the better. Thus, they will need to know the type of location that you are looking for in order to effectively narrow their search. If you don't know, be honest about the overall budget and what this needs to include so that they will be able to work out roughly what allocation would be available for the location in order to accurately undertake their investigations.

Conversely, if you would like to undertake your own location search, there are four/five key avenues to explore:

1) Trade books/CD ROM
2) Tourist board

★ Pre booked generally means that the agency commission will be based in relation to the details originally featured on the contract, whilst some locations also allow for any subsequent amendments made to the contract prior to the event date.

3) The Internet
4) Word of mouth

or

5) Head/Sales Office

Firstly, there are many ways to investigate locations when sourcing from trade publications but two of my personal favourite sources of information have always been the Blue & Green Book and Johansens. These informative, quality reference books and CD ROM's enable you to easily identify hotel and venue suitability in terms of location, size, style and facilities.

Secondly, depending upon the region I am researching, I also like to contact the relevant tourist board and ask them to forward their Convention Book/Location Directory which details all hotels and venues that can host corporate events within its area.

Thirdly, with the innovation of the Internet, so came with this impressive communication tool, the facility for the most *novice* of event organisers to undertake thorough location searches. It should be said that also found on the internet are 'associations'. These bodies can help to identify locations that fulfil certain criteria. (See Helpful Contact Details.)

Fourthly, colleagues, friends and even local reporters always have something to say about their experiences of attending events at a variety of locations – why not be bold and just ask their opinion. If someone has had a dreadful experience at a location (although it doesn't always follow that you will also receive a similar negative experience) you may find that you automatically place this location on your 'B' list, saving time and energy to concentrate on locations that are to be placed firmly on your 'A', to investigate further, list.

There is a fifth option, should you wish to host your event with an hotel, and that is to contact the Head/Sales Office of the major hotel chains. Some favour this option as each Sales Office will contact all relevant hotels within its chain and, basically, undertake all the leg work for you. I prefer to contact hotels on an individual basis, but it is purely down to personal choice.

Top Tip Tick:

There is a sixth and important option but it is not always accessible to 'non trade' and that is to attend exhibitions. Exhibitions, such as Event UK (previously the National Venue Show) that focus on promoting locations in the UK whilst Confex exhibits locations in both the UK and overseas. Both encourage the attendance of anyone who organises an event whether the person is an existing event organiser, personal assistant, executive assistant, secretary or of management status within a company. My advice would be to visit exhibition websites to establish whether there are any limiting factors for attendees or whether 'all' are welcome. (Website details feature in Helpful Contact Details.)

Keep a List

So, whichever path you choose to identify potential locations, after establishing a number of options, write a secondary list of those that you feel are worth contacting – your 'A' list if you like. Constantly refer to the Event Brief to keep in mind the objectives of the event and see if any locations in particular jump out at you as being a potential winner. The locations that, on paper, seem to best fulfil the brief are the ones to be placed on to your 'A' list.

Here are a few more pointers:

Allow ample time

If you are undertaking the location search yourself, this is quite a laborious task and you should set aside anything up to five days in which to complete the initial search and document the responses.

Whom do you contact?

When contacting a location, ask to speak to a representative in the conference and banqueting department.

Once a contact has been established, I find that it is always best to email across a written brief, which is typed either on letterhead or features all contact details so that it is very clear to the person in question *where* and *whom* to contact when they formally respond.

Top Tip Tick:

Always, always ask for the location's suitability and quote to be sent in writing. That way, if there are ever any questions or conflict in the future, everything is in black and white. If you receive information by telephone, confirm your understanding back in writing and ask them to respond as to whether your understanding is correct or indeed incorrect. It's better to be safe than sorry.

Redefine the Brief

In order for the location to confirm its suitability and costings, the hotel or venue need to be informed of some key information and, as such, I tend to create a Location Brief which is basically a tweaked version of the Event Brief document.

The information that you are trying to establish is whether the location is suitable, whether it is available and how much it will cost? Hence, the location needs to receive some key, factual, information.

Referring to our fictional scenario, take a moment to complete this document with the information that you feel a location would need to know whilst utilising the following headings as featured, in part, on the original Event Brief:

Location Brief

Event:

Location:

Date:

Guests:

Requirements:

Time:

Theme:

Vision:

Accommodation:

Objective:

Pre requisite:

Please confirm the following:

-

-

-

-

-

-

-

-

The following Location Brief includes the information that I would incorporate. How did your Location Brief compare? Your descriptions may, of course, vary from mine and don't worry if you inadvertently missed out any key information – by the time you have finished this book, you will be thinking like a proficient event organiser so these clarifications and questions will, eventually, readily spring to mind.

Location Brief

Event:	Party
Location:	Central London
Date:	July 24th
Guests:	200 x guests
Requirements:	Drinks reception Dinner (formal) Dancing and entertainment
Time:	19.30 – midnight
Theme:	French
Vision:	4★ event (but with 5★ service and style)
Accommodation:	Required for 10 x single occupancy rooms, plus additional rooms may be booked direct by guests wishing to stay overnight
Objective:	A celebration and a thank you to clients
Pre requisite:	Flexibility – wish to enhance the overall experience with the theme which may include food, drink etc.

Please confirm the following:

- Your availability?

- Confirmation of the suitability of your location and the function rooms/areas that you would suggest utilising?

- Whether there are any restrictions which may have some bearing on the event?

- Your maximum capacity for the layout required?

- Whether there is anything in particular your location could offer when considering a theme of this nature?

- The costs associated with this event?

- Agency commission? (if applicable)

- Whether costs are inclusive or exclusive of VAT?

When you receive a response, this will help to gauge how suitable the location is for your particular needs. In particular, when enquiring if there are any 'restrictions', this will determine whether adhering to limitations will curtail any element of the event. For example: if selecting a location that is within a residential area, the location may request that the event organiser (and any relevant suppliers) adhere to a code of conduct. This code is normally compiled to ensure that disruption to residents is kept to the minimum. As the event organiser, you would normally be obliged to comply with strict load in and load out timings, parking and traffic monitoring along with limiting the level of sound for recorded or live music – so, it is always worthwhile checking on any restrictions at this early stage.

Top Tip Tick:

If a location is available and is deemed suitable for your requirements, place the date/location on 'provisional hold'. This is the equivalent of 'pencilling in a date'. The location will hold this date without commitment until the requirement can be formally confirmed or until the location receives another enquiry for the provisional date you have held. In which case, the location will provide a date by which you or the brief provider will need to confirm the event or release.

You may hear the term 'first' or 'second' option. If the location informs you that the space can be provisionally held on 'first' option this means that you are the first in the queue and there are presently no other interested parties. If the location states that space will be held on 'second' option this means that someone else is presently holding the same date. The location will confirm the terms that you could move up to first option i.e. the party presently holding has been given a deadline by which to confirm their event or whoever confirms first will be assigned the date(s).

Charges

When organising an event which takes place during the day and/or follows through to an evening affair, you should ask the location to confirm their day delegate rate (DDR) or, if guests are staying overnight, their 24 hour delegate rate.

The day delegate rate normally includes the following main aspects:

- Main function room hire (during event timings and where guests are present)
- Morning and afternoon refreshments (2 or 3 servings depending upon hotel/venue)
- Lunch

24 Hour Delegate Rate would also include:

- Dinner
- Bed and breakfast

However, if you require an evening event, such as the type of function specified for the fictional brief, the location is likely to charge a room hire and separate catering cost or a dinner rate that includes room hire.

Top Tip Tick:

As some venues do not have accommodation on site, their costing structure may be different to a Delegate Rate i.e. they will charge room hire along with food and beverage separately. However, some venues or hotels will not charge room hire if there is a large number of guests attending. It is advisable, if a room hire charge is levied, to enquire if the location will negotiate on this aspect of their quote. Indeed, it is always advisable to see if there are any circumstances in which they will negotiate on their rates across the board. Well, if you don't ask, you certainly won't get.

Administrative Housekeeping

As you receive quotes from various locations, you will undoubtedly start to generate and accumulate lots of pieces of paper and emails. Soon enough, these will be sprawled over your work top or desk – so now is the time to open your Event Organiser's File.

Obviously, you will manage your computer files as you deem fit, regardless of your computer and everyday administrative 'housekeeping' methods. (Not to be confused with the term associated with a hotel, although there are some similarities.) Good administrative housekeeping is all about keeping your files in order and administration up together.

I know that the following suggestion may seem a little antiquated but in order to track and monitor information easily, promptly and reliably you may wish to follow how I worked for many years and that is to print out every document and work from a hard copy file.

Printing out all documents is by far the best way of keeping totally abreast of the pre production phase but, ecologically, I found myself questioning this method more and more and no matter how many trees I contributed towards to be replanted, I felt that there had to be a better way forward. A few years ago I addressed the issue of utilising copious amounts of paper and cartridges by limiting myself to just printing out key documents but actioning emails as they arrived to ensure that I kept on top of the organisational process.

This change of practice was timely as November 2007 saw the publication of BS 8901 – Specification for a Sustainable Event Management System. The Standard provides requirements for planning and managing 'sustainable' events and is applicable throughout the industry to event organisers, clients, venues and organisations or individuals in the supply chain. Although as a Standard it is not obligatory, in this day and age, I personally feel that we should all consider how we can 'do our bit' to create events that are environmentally friendly – communicating by email, reducing the amount of paperwork generated and recycling when considering the task of administrative housekeeping; it can all help. (To obtain your copy of BS 8901, please see Helpful Contact Details.)

So let us assume that you will also be opting for the more space efficient and environmentally friendly way of organising the event and you err towards printing out only key documents…

Get yourself an A4 hard bound lever arch file along with some section dividers. Also place in the front of your file an A4 To Do List Sheet and Extra Costs Sheet. The index headings on the section dividers can change for each event requirement but, generally, I would suggest you create your file whilst incorporating the following headings:

- To Boss/Colleague/Client (whoever is the brief provider)
- From Boss/Colleague/Client
- To Location
- From Location
- To Supplier(s) (these can be broken down into sub headings depending upon the number of suppliers being utilised for the whole event)
- From Supplier(s) as above
- Costings
- Contracts/Agreements
- Notes

Top Tip Tick:

There are a number of software programmes on the market to assist with the organisational process of an event. Although these can indeed be helpful, I find that it is best to first have a basic understanding at grass root level prior to moving on to any computer software support. When you are thinking like a proficient event organiser, then you can draw upon additional support mechanisms.

Document Management

For all emails/letters that you feel are of sufficient importance to print out, file each document within the various appropriate sections. For those that require a response or an action, place the document (or copy) at the very front of the file. Only when suppliers have responded or you have actioned, do you place the original document and the response(s) into the main body of the folder. This way, at a glance, you can see from whom you are awaiting a key response or what action you still need to undertake. (This document management process should be consistent for all documentation, regardless of whom it is addressed *to* or *from*.)

This process can be mirrored on your computer – only file away an email when you have received a response or actioned a reply.

Also, if a supplier or the brief provider has asked a question and you are waiting to action it, keep this note, email or letter in the same manner and only file away into the relevant section of the folder when actioned. Again, this helps with the event organisation process. Tidy file/computer, tidy 'relaxed' mind!

Top Tip Tick:

What constitutes an 'important' document? Any document that clarifies a costing, specific confirmation of action, contract, agreement, clarification to/from a supplier or the brief provider. Namely, any key document that needs easy access in the form of a hard copy.

To Do List & Extra Costs Sheet

You may wake up in the morning and remember something that you need to do or you could be on the phone and something springs to mind… use the A4 To Do List at the front of your file to write anything down that you wish to remember. When you have actioned the task, highlight it so you know it has been done.

(The Extra Costs Sheet is for use under similar circumstances as the To Do List. It is a reminder sheet of any changes that arise, and there will be many, subsequent to the initial costing innovation and during the course of the organisation, that have a bearing on the overall event costing. When you have incorporated this amendment into the body of the ongoing spreadsheet, the element can be highlighted off the sheet.)

This is the start of 'ticking off the list' – the more highlighting you achieve, the happier you will feel.

Guideline Costing

So, you are now hopefully in receipt of some location options. Your next step is to create a guideline costing (Event Costing).

I normally utilise a spreadsheet for this purpose and this is where the mindset of a proficient event organiser truly comes into play. (I also tend to add the acronym E&OE to the spreadsheet, this is just to clarify that the costs have been calculated to the best of my ability and any Errors and Omissions are to be Excepted.)

Visualisation

I have previously mentioned about trying to *think* like a proficient event organiser. When you get to this stage, it's all about *visualisation*.

The best way to contemplate an event from beginning to end is to quite simply visualise every step of the way.

Think of the fictional event we are together contemplating. What questions do you immediately think of when considering the complete function?

To demonstrate what I mean, I am visualising myself as a guest arriving at the event. Now, I walk through the event which in itself raises many a question… Don your 'guest' hat once again and join me on the visualisation journey. (Some are relevant for costing purposes, others will be relevant for organisational purposes.)

- How do I know about the event?
- What should I wear?
- Do I know where it is?
- What are the timings of the event?
- How am I going to get there?
- Will there be somewhere to leave my coat?
- What is the format of the event?
- When I get there what will I do?
- Will there be drinks and nibbles upon arrival?
- Will I have to pay for my drinks?
- When I get there what will I see?
- When I get there what will I hear?
- Will I be sitting down to eat or standing up informally?
- Will I be sitting where I like or will there be a formal table plan?
- Will they have taken into account my special dietary requirement?
- Will I be having wine with my meal?
- What will the tables and the main dining room look like?
- Will there be entertainment during dinner?
- Will I need to pay for drinks after dinner?

- What can I drink after dinner?
- Will there be entertainment after dinner?
- How will I get home?

Similar questions relating specifically to each event will always need to be asked – when you start to build your event content this will, at the same time, help with the costing and general organisation process. Therefore, visualising and asking yourself questions of this nature are REALLY IMPORTANT and this visualisation step should never be skipped.

Spreadsheet Headings

Now is the time to start placing the headings on to your Event Costing spreadsheet in sequential order on how the event runs and taking into account the questions that we have just asked above. For example:

Let us look at the first question. *How do I know about this event? This question lends itself to considering:*
The invitation

How am I going to get there? This question lends itself to considering:
The transportation

And so on and so forth. By donning your 'event organiser' hat, try to establish the aspects of an event which should be considered when contemplating the questions above.

Overleaf are the spreadsheet headings that I would consider for this particular fictional event… based on the visualisation exercise.

Event Costing			
Invitation			
Transportation			
Location/room hire			
Pre dinner drinks			
Canapés			
Floral décor/theming (pre dinner)			
Entertainment during pre dinner drinks			
Table plan etc			
Place cards			
Dinner			
Dinner drinks			
Table centres			
Theming of main room			
Entertainment during dinner			
Entertainment after dinner			
DJ			
Accommodation (management staff)			
Contingency (inc cloakroom attendant)			

NB: You will see that I have added a contingency element as, at this very early stage of the planning, you will not have worked out any logistics so a healthy contingency is always advisable for any miscellaneous aspects that you will need to organise/provide as the event is developed. As such, until an aspect of the event such as the cloakroom attendant can be fully considered, it is best to place an element of this nature within a Contingency heading.

The second spreadsheet features some costing allocations. I believe that this is the best way to get a true feel of the event whilst working towards a budget. You may recall that the budget was £140.00 per head and there were anticipated to be 200 guests, providing a total budget of £28,000.00 plus VAT. Imagining I utilised the costs I received from an 'A' list hotel, I started allocating a) specific, where costs could be confirmed at this stage i.e. from the hotel and b) general allocations, where costs were not known.

Event Costing (E&OE)	No:	Per person	Total
Invitation			£500.00
Transportation			n/a
Location/room hire			£2,500.00
Pre dinner drinks	200	£10.00	£2,000.00
Canapés	200	£4.00	£800.00
Floral décor/theming (pre dinner drinks)			£1,000.00
Entertainment during pre dinner drinks			£1,000.00
Table plan etc			£200.00
Place cards			£200.00
Dinner	200	£35.00	£7,000.00
Dinner drinks	200	£10.00	£2,000.00
Table centres	25	£50.00	£1,250.00
Theming of main room			£2,000.00
Entertainment during dinner			£1,000.00
Entertainment after dinner			£1,750.00
DJ			£800.00
Accommodation (management staff)	10	£150.00	£1,500.00
Contingency (inc cloakroom attendant)			£2,500.00
Total			**£28,000.00**

Top Tip Tick:

When contemplating room hire costs, always bear in mind whether you anticipate needing some set up time to prepare the main room for erecting audio visual equipment, rehearsals, theming etc. Remember to ensure that all the rooms that you need access to are indeed available for set up when initially requesting availability and feature this request on the Location Brief - also remember to include this element and costing ramification into your Event Costing spreadsheet.

The Event Costing example demonstrates the elements coming in within budget but my first guestimation of costs transpired to be £2,400.00 over budget. How did you do? I played around with the allocations so I could obtain a feel of the costs I would need to secure from the various suppliers in order to bring this fictional event in within budget.

By undertaking a guideline costing of this nature, you will soon be able to identify the anticipated elements that could be organised within the budget. You will be able to identify from your 'A' list the location that best suits the budget whilst some of your options will be eliminated purely because of budgetary factors. All of which will help to narrow down the options.

Top Tip Tick:

When considering costs you need to ascertain, for a function similar to our fictional event, the table configuration for the anticipated number of guests. Rule of thumb. A five foot round banqueting table will sit eight guests comfortably. In my opinion, ten guests on a table of this size are a little tight.

When the location confirms that it can accommodate this number of guests, always ask what size tables they provide and how many guests they have allocated per table. Further, ask them to provide a floor plan indicating the layout they are suggesting - there is nothing worse than guests feeling that they have been squeezed on to a table or, indeed, into a room so, best to check first.

Likewise, should you be organising a conference, you should always request the location to forward floor plans, specifying how they visualise seating your maximum amount of guests in the layout requested i.e. theatre style, cabaret etc.

Update Time

Now that you have undertaken a search, short listed the locations and created a guideline costing, it's a good time to seek some feedback from the brief provider.

If he/she is happy in particular with the elements that you intend to include within the budget and the location options, the next stage is to undertake a site visit to the short listed locations. (You may, however, have one location, in particular, you wish to visit prior to concentrating on any of the other short listed locations. This is perfectly understandable, as site visits are extremely time consuming.)

You will need to once again communicate with your designated point of contact at the location(s) to arrange a site visit. Prior to making this call or email try to identify more than one date and time that the site visit can take place as the location will need to make certain that the areas that you will potentially be using are available to view. Try to give as much notice as possible in order to organise this site visit so that you can get the most out of the inspection.

Top Tip Tick:

Do be aware that the location's aim is to sell their facilities and if they manage to confirm an event which utilises your anticipated areas prior to the site visit– these facilities may cease to become available for inspection. Ask the location to notify you should this situation arise in order to reschedule the site visit.

Site Visit

Prior to setting off on your site visit, make sure that you are well prepared. Take an A4 pad and pen, a digital camera, a copy of the details/quote that the location forwarded to you along with, of course, the original Event Brief and Location Brief.

On the way to the location, be aware of your surroundings and again wear your 'guest' hat. How easy was it to find this place? Constantly keep asking yourself questions – visualise yourself as a guest arriving at the location. Where can I park? Are there ample parking spaces? What about trains or bus routes?

When you enter the location, consciously register how you felt when you arrived – were you pleased with what you saw? Were you excited or did the location leave you cold? Write down your thoughts every step of the way.

As you walk into the location, note if you were greeted warmly and whether it was easy to get your bearings? When you approached reception, again, were you greeted courteously and expediently? Did you have to wait long for someone to meet you? All these tell tale signs are a good indication of how your function, if you chose this location, would be dealt with.

When the representative from the conference and banqueting department greets and shows you around the areas she/he is proposing you utilise, whilst referring to the Event and Location Brief continue to visualise yourself as a guest and take photographs of the rooms you view. Are you happy with what you see and experience?

Top Tip Tick:

When on your site visit, take a moment to look below eye level. Is there wallpaper peeling by the skirting boards? Is there dust on the window sills? Are there dirty coffee cups lying around? I always feel that if a location takes care of its property and displays excellent housekeeping, this is a good indication that the event you are organising will be treated in the same impeccable manner.

During the initial site visit is a good time to establish whether the location has any 'sustainability' measures in place. These could be simple things such as whether they provide fresh, seasonal produce sourced from local suppliers? Whether they are registered with the Green Tourism Business Scheme? If they have a member of staff or team responsible for environmental management and whether they practice waste minimisation and have recycling facilities. Although many locations may not yet have sustainability measures in place, it's worth asking the question to highlight the demand and, hopefully, to encourage change. Also, ask some miscellaneous details such as (should you be visiting a hotel) whether complimentary newspapers are provided for anyone staying overnight? Whether mini-bars are fully stocked in bedrooms? And, very importantly, clarification of when the fire alarm tests are scheduled?

Remember to also check on whether any business facilities are available and the costs associated with these services and if there are any specific dress codes that the guests would need to comply with.

Top Tip Tick:

When visiting a hotel and being shown a bedroom, always ask to see the good, the bad and the ugly! This way you will know what the best and worst case scenario could be. If the 'worst' bedroom has been titled as such due to, say, its size and location rather than condition/style of bedroom, ask if all bedrooms are of the same standard as the rooms that you were shown.

Be sure to request the standard and position of bedrooms that you would like the guests to be assigned, should you bring the business to them. Also, request the location confirms that it is able to accommodate your wishes.

When you are happy that you have seen everything you need to and, if not requested previously, make certain that you obtain two corporate packs. (One for you and one for the brief provider.) The packs should contain: pictures of facilities, all room dimensions, delegate menus, drink tariffs, clarification of exactly what is included in the various delegate rates or costing structure, transport link details and directions/maps – all of which will be helpful to you at a later stage.

NB: It should be mentioned that if you are undertaking a site visit which is some distance away from where you live or work and, if you are inspecting a hotel, the location should be able to provide overnight accommodation (subject to availability). Depending upon the policy of the hotel, they may provide bed and breakfast on a complimentary basis or charge a discounted rate that will be deducted off the main bill should the event be confirmed at a later stage.

Top Tip Tick:

Although the most environmentally friendly option is to create natural airflow, always ask about air conditioning. Sometimes a room can become very hot when there is a set present or theming in place. When combined with lots of guests (should the room not have large opening windows) air conditioning is a must. Also, when considering the general wellbeing of guests, identify whether there are any outside areas (should the event be taking place during the warm months) to take refreshments as guests always like access to some fresh air and smokers appreciate the respite.

Finally, take a moment to register if your mobile phone signal is strong within all of the function rooms that are potentially being used, in particular where you would be based i.e. a production office. Generally make sure that there is a phone with an outside line available and enquire regarding broadband/internet facilities including WIFI capability.

Costing Update

Now you have seen the available location(s), you may like to consider your findings and undertake some costing comparisons if you haven't done so before. Utilising the guideline costing spreadsheet, insert the costs for each of the locations that are of greatest interest.

You will now have in your possession a range of costing options based on a variety of locations and hopefully identified which is your preferred location. Prior to making the final selection, this is the time when you should try to negotiate further on costs quoted just to establish if there is any additional leeway. (You can always make each location aware that you are seriously considering its premises and they are firmly on the 'shortlist' to hopefully encourage some movement.) If they come back with a revised offer, place these revised costs into your Event Costing spreadsheet.

Top Tip Tick:

Most but not all locations charge their costs on an 'inclusive' of VAT basis, whilst most suppliers charge for their service 'exclusive' of VAT. It is important that when reaching this stage i.e. updating your initial guideline costing with accurate location costs that you remain consistent.

Always check with locations, should their costs be 'inclusive' of VAT, that ALL costs quoted are inclusive as some aspects such as room hire are sometimes VAT Zero Rated. Assuming that all of the location costs do include VAT, I calculate and utilise the net figure, then these figures will correspond with all the suppliers' figures. Ensure that the brief provider is aware that the costs featured on the spreadsheet are 'plus' VAT.

There is one exception to this rule and that is if the company or client that you are working on behalf of is not VAT registered. You would need to ensure that all the costs that you feature are 'inclusive' rather than 'exclusive' of VAT. Under these circumstances, it may be advisable to take accountancy advice when initially setting up the costing aspect.

Authorisation

This is the perfect time to request a meeting with the brief provider and to express to him/her your feeling as to the location which would, in your opinion, be best suited to the event and, indeed, budget. Produce your updated Event Costing, which features the accurate costs from your preferred location but still has 'allocations' for the rest of the costings, so that all the facts known to date are to hand. Ensure that you also provide a copy of the location's Corporate Pack and present any additional or relevant photographs taken during the site visit.

At this stage, the brief provider may take your advice or wish to personally see your proposed location prior to giving the go-ahead. If this is the case, you will need to arrange for a secondary site visit to the location. When you do so, make sure that you inform the establishment well in advance of all the areas that you wish to visit and arrange your preferred schedule directly with them.

Top Tip Tick:

When the brief provider authorises you to confirm and proceed with the organisation of the event, make sure that you receive this authorisation in writing prior to confirming the location – even if this person is a work colleague. This way, should there be any conflict, you can prove that you were working under instruction and proceeded on this basis.

Confirmation

So now you have gained the authorisation to proceed, the next step is to formally confirm the location. Once you have the location secured, this will be when you can start to relax and take your time (should time allow) to contemplate fully the content of the event and how you can best utilise the overall event budget.

When you confirm the location, always, always do so in writing!

Ensure that you reiterate your key understanding which should include:

- Date of event
- Name of function rooms utilised
- Number of bedrooms required, position and standard expected (if applicable)
- Approx number of guests
- Guideline timings of event (including set up and actual event)
- Confirm agreement of costs and whether they include or exclude VAT
- Provide details of the person responsible for signing the contract and issuing payment
- Confirm who you understand the contact to be at the location

---

Top Tip Tick:

Should you need to confirm any bedroom requirements, forward to the location an accommodation spreadsheet in 'pecking order' if you are in the position to do so at this early stage. This will mean that those guests who should be allocated the best rooms will be prioritised accordingly. (When discussing accommodation requirements, always check to see if the hotel will offer any complimentary upgrades plus whether it will provide any special touches such as chocolates, fruit or flowers for any key guests.)

Contract

Once your letter of confirmation has been received, the location will undoubtedly wish to go to formal contract expeditiously.

When you receive the Contract, carefully read through the details featured to make sure that they are as you have previously agreed and understood. If not, go back to the location so that they can rectify this and, where necessary, raise a revised Contract.

Depending upon the circumstance, you, your boss, colleague or client may wish to sign the Contract. Just ensure that whoever is undertaking this task is authorised to do so, especially if signing 'on behalf' of a company thereby becoming 'the contracting party'.

Part of the Contract will be the location's terms and conditions. My advice to all my clients is simple. If in doubt, seek legal advice prior to signing anything. If, conversely, you have a query which is not so much a legality but more of an *understanding* issue, seek further clarification with the location and where applicable, request amendments.

Top Tip Tick:

Location's terms and conditions are all different. There are, however, normally two key clauses that you may like to consider and discuss in detail with the location prior to the contract being signed. There will probably be one clause which relates to function room usage. Locations normally include a clause allowing them to change the agreed function room without the client's prior authorisation – although this is, in my opinion, perfectly acceptable should they experience a problem that cannot be overcome i.e. there is a flood in the room and if the function you are organising were not moved then the event could not go ahead. It is, nevertheless, always worth clarifying the circumstances that they would envisage undertaking this action whilst at the same time making it known that you would not accept a room exchange if it wasn't under extenuating circumstances. For example, if the hotel had double booked then, to me, this is not a good enough reason to swap your room. Believe you me, it can happen.

This is even more relevant when you are organising a themed event or, indeed, a conference. All your theming and/or conference set will have been designed to fit within a specific room so hence the reason why a change of room would be unacceptable.

The second potential clause which is worth discussing at greater length relates to minimum numbers. Some locations will base the contract on minimum numbers; for example for an event where you are expecting 400 guests, the location may allow for a 10% leeway and base the contract on a minimum number of 360 guests. This would mean that if only 300 guests attend, they may still charge for 360.

It is essential to ask at the outset for the maximum capacity of a room just to ensure that if the maximum number of guests wished to attend i.e. 400, then they can still fit in the room but at the same time ask the location what minimum number of guests they would accept to guarantee the use of that particular room? They may say 300 guests and as such, you reduce the risk of unnecessary penalties if you ask the location to base the contract on the minimum with a view to being able to increase numbers up to the maximum at a later date.

Within a location's terms and conditions there should be details of cancellation policies, a payment section which outlines payment schedules (whether deposits are required and when stage payments are due) along with a credit application form - request an application form if not featured within the body of the document. My advice is to read these details very carefully and draw these clauses, if relevant, to the attention of the person signing the contract and authorising payments.

One final word of advice. Until the Contract has been signed by both parties, nothing can be guaranteed. Wait for this important document to be finalised prior to informing any key personnel or actioning any requirement such as sending out invitations, among others – a lot can happen in-between contract signing and you don't want to end up with egg on your face.

With this in mind, unless another location (which you may also have on provisional hold) has an alternative client who wishes to confirm an event on your specified date(s), try to delay formally releasing any other location until you, your boss, colleague or client have received a signed contract from the chosen location. Then again, if you are chased by an alternative location prior to receiving the exchanged contract, do have the grace to release your provisional hold to provide the location with the opportunity to resell the date. Regardless of the time frame, always take a moment to release all provisional holds – it's just good manners.

So to recap then….during your early days as a proficient event organiser, you have managed to undertake the following:

- Identify and clarify the objectives of an event
- Source a range of potential locations
- Undertake a site visit(s)
- Create some guideline costings
  and
- Formally confirm a location

Great, you are well on your way. You can shortly start to contemplate the overall event design, but first…let's look at the organisational process of this pre production phase.

CHAPTER 2

Pre Production – Organisation

Pre Production – Organisation

Now that the location has been secured, the time has come to concentrate on some further administrative housekeeping.

There are two main aspects to this next stage and those are the creation of two key organisational documents, namely: The Itinerary and the Benchmark Schedule.

The Itinerary

I mentioned previously that I would introduce you to my 'event bible' or the Event Itinerary. I am famous for my Event Itineraries!

What is an Event Itinerary?

In a nutshell, it is the complete understanding, organisation and management of an event pulled together in one document. It is created so that whilst working on site, at a glance, everything that has been organised can be viewed, details of what anyone should be doing at that particular time have been clarified and future tasks identified.

It is a document that you, any event team and location banqueting staff work from to ensure that all the various personnel dovetail their management process.

It is, quite simply, a gem of a document!

Getting Started

Taking on board the fictional event... unbeknown to yourself, you have already constructed the bones of an itinerary – it's the information as stated on the original Event Brief and as discussed/confirmed *to* and *from* the location.

Start by placing this information in a simple Word document. The layout being something like this...

Itinerary

Friday 24th July:

08.00 Main function room (The Palace Suite) access available for set up.
   (Discounted to £1,800.00 inc VAT – all hotel costs are quoted inclusive of VAT i.e. £1,531.92 plus VAT★.)

   Max. capacity for the main function room is 300 x guests in total. (Floor plan obtained based on maximum.)

   Min. capacity to safeguard the main function room is 150 guests.
   Hotel provides 5' rounds for dining and allows for 8 x guests per table.

   Air conditioning is available in the main function room. (Natural daylight and large windows also in situ.)
   WIFI is not available. An outside line and Broadband is available in the Production Office. Good mobile phone coverage throughout hotel.

   No particular dress code applies to corporate guests.

   Business facilities are available in the Business Lounge. (Charged upon consumption.)

   The hotel's French chef is available for this function.

10.00 Fire Alarm testing takes place. (No evacuation needed.)

19.30 Guests arrive. (Approx 200.)

   All guests arriving under their own steam. (Ample car parking – free of charge.)
   Local tube and mainline station are 5 and 10 mins walking distance respectively.

   Smoking is allowed outside on the terrace.

---

*VAT is calculated at 17.5% throughout this book

Pre dinner drinks take place in the Tower Suite. (No charge for room hire, complimentary.)

Glass of house champagne is from £6.00 inc VAT (£5.11 plus VAT).
Glass of house wine is from £4.95 inc VAT (£4.21 plus VAT).
Canapés commence from £4.00 inc VAT (£3.40 plus VAT).

20.15   Guests moved into dinner (The Palace Suite).

20.30   Dinner is served.

Menu commences from £39.00 inc VAT (£33.19 plus VAT). Wines commence from £13.95 per bottle inc VAT (£11.87 plus VAT). (Produce is sourced locally where feasible and menus utilise produce in season.)

21.30   Entertainment commences.

22.00   Dancing commences.

M'night   Event ceases – guests depart.

Accommodation:

10 x single occupancy rooms (booked). B&B rate of £150.00 inc VAT per person (£127.66 plus VAT).

Mini bars are fully stocked. Complimentary newspapers are provided.

Information (working file)

When you formally confirm a location, from hereon in, I would recommend that an itinerary document is kept up and running whenever working on any aspect of the event. I mentioned previously that I used to print out all forms of correspondence and only when the necessary action had been undertaken was the document filed away into its relevant section – this also follows when importing information into an itinerary.

By keeping an itinerary document live, whenever a question is raised by the brief provider, this question is to be written into the Itinerary. Should a location answer a question that you have posed, the answer is written into the Itinerary and so on. Look upon your Itinerary as an extension of your existing To Do List - they really work hand in hand with each other.

Since amending my administration practices, I now actually work from two computer screens. One screen is solely dedicated to an event itinerary whilst the other is utilised as normal for compiling, sending and receiving emails and correspondence.

Top Tip Tick:

Persevere. Although it may seem a somewhat laborious task (especially for the most novice of event organisers) to reiterate and input information into one document, with ease you will be able to know at any time during the organisational process which supplier is yet to confirm responses, who has requested a clarification, rates etc. This saves you rifling around a file and your email inbox/outbox trying to frantically find the answer to many questions that will undoubtedly arise. It saves time, it keeps your mind relaxed and you know exactly where you are on a daily basis.

Questions

After you have imported all the key facts from your existing working file, whilst thinking like a proficient event organiser and donning your 'guest' hat, if you have any additional questions that spring to mind, simply write them into this document.

When considering the fictional event, at this stage you would need to ask yourself questions like… 'I've seen a floor plan for 300 guests, what will the room look like with 200 guests?

Next, write an action like …. 'Ask hotel to provide a floor plan based on 200 guests' and write this and any other similar question in red. And so on, until you have concluded your questions and actions to date. This is the start of your organisation with the location. This will be the first of many questions you will ask the location (and where applicable, suppliers) during the course of the pre production phase.

Top Tip Tick:

For easy identification of tasks to do within an itinerary, I like to colour code. For example:

Confirmation/statement of details:	*Black*
Questions or duties of event organiser to action:	*Red*
Questions raised/answers waiting from brief provider:	*Blue*
Questions raised/ answers waiting from location:	*Green*
Questions raised/answers waiting from suppliers:	*Purple*

When you receive an answer and that particular task has been organised, revert the question back to 'black' and collate the information into statement form, similar to all the factual information already incorporated into the Itinerary which was based on contracted details from the location of our fictional event.

Basically, what you are trying to achieve is that all key information stored either within your working file or within your computer filing system, features within the Itinerary document so there is no need when on site to constantly refer to the working file(s) or your laptop to refresh your memory of the discussions that have taken place and agreed between all parties.

The example Itinerary overleaf is a development of the initial document and demonstrates how best to apply the questions and thought process as you continue on your organisational quest. (Identified by the use of bold and italics.)

Itinerary

Friday 24th July:

08.00   Main function room (The Palace Suite) access available for set up.
(Discounted to £1,800.00 inc VAT – all hotel costs are quoted inclusive of VAT ie £1,531.92 plus VAT.)

Max. capacity for the main function room is 300 x guests in total. (Floor plan obtained based on maximum.) *Ask hotel to provide a floor plan based on 200 x guests.*

Min. capacity to safeguard the main function room is 150 guests.
Hotel provides 5' rounds for dining and allow for 8 x guests per table.

Have asked Lilly if she anticipates wanting a top table?

Air conditioning is available in the main function room. (Natural daylight and large windows also in situ.) WIFI is not available. An outside line and broadband is avail in the Production Office. Good mobile coverage throughout the hotel.

No particular dress code applies to corporate guests.

Business facilities are available in the Business Lounge. (Charged upon consumption.)

Asked hotel the cost for photocopying and printing.

The hotel's French chef is available for this function.

Hotel have requested whether anticipate wanting a French menu or traditional English? To consider this and respond when further contemplated overall theme.

10.00   Fire Alarm testing takes place. (No evacuation needed.)

19.30   Guests arrive. (Approx. 200.)

All guests arriving under their own steam. (Ample car parking – free of charge.)
Local tube and mainline station are 5 and 10 mins walking distance respectively.
Find out more details about public transport and how many car parking spaces there are available.

Noticed when undertook site visit that the hotel toilets were quite far from the function rooms, have asked if there are any closer toilet facilities?

Smoking is allowed outside on the terrace.

Pre dinner drinks take place in the Tower Suite. (No charge for room hire, complimentary.)

Glass of house champagne is from £6.00 inc VAT (£5.11 plus VAT).
Glass of house wine is from £4.95 inc VAT (£4.21 plus VAT).
Canapés commence from £4.00 inc VAT (£3.40 plus VAT).

20.15   Guests moved into dinner (The Palace Suite).

Dinner is served.

Menu commences from £39.00 inc VAT (£33.19 plus VAT.) Wine commences from £13.95 inc VAT (£11.87 plus VAT). (Produce is sourced locally where feasible and menus utilise produce in season.)

21.30   Entertainment commences.

To arrange for a cash bar.

Dancing commences.

M'night Event ceases – guests depart.

Accommodation:

10 x single occupancy rooms (booked). B&B rate of £150.00 inc VAT per person (£127.66 plus VAT).

Forward a pecking order rooming list to hotel when known.

Mini bars are fully stocked. Complimentary newspapers are provided.

Top Tip Tick:

It is essential that the order of the information featured in the Itinerary is kept in accordance with the schedule of the event i.e. if you are detailing guests' arrival, make sure that any relevant information features within the time frame stated rather than ad hoc which would be hard to follow when working on site.

Keep expanding on the Itinerary throughout the organisational process until you have created a complete document. At this point in time the document will not include much, if any, 'logistical' information. That comes at a later stage. The final Itinerary will include all aspects including the number of guests attending, menus selected, accommodation, logistical and organisational processes.

You will find that the second key document, the Benchmark Schedule, which we discuss below, will also throw up a great number of questions. Incorporate these questions into the Itinerary, as the Itinerary becomes your premier 'to do list'.

At the end of this book (Chapter 13) a complete Itinerary can be viewed based on the fictional event just to give an indication of the level of information which should feature within this very helpful document. (Details can be similarly replicated for all manner of events.)

The Benchmark Schedule

The Benchmark Schedule is a document based on a time line and will help you and indeed any organisation team, to manage the workload in bite sized chunks whilst fulfilling any deadlines.

The Benchmark Schedule is created on a landscape spreadsheet and I start by, quite simply, listing the available weeks from commencement of the Schedule to the event date itself and this takes the form of a weekly diary chart..

The first column should be allocated to 'Weekly Dates', the second to 'Action Required', the third to 'Person Responsible for Actioning', whilst the fourth column should be allocated for 'Action Status'.

When you have created your template and added all the dates between commencement and the event date, then you can start building your Benchmark Schedule.

The first set of dates and deadlines to add to your schedule is based on the location Contract and their terms and conditions of business. Read through the document and add important information such as: payment terms/dates, cancellation charges, rooming list provision, catering numbers, special dietary needs notification and date when function layout plans need to be submitted - should you be staging a conference or similar and the location requests this information to ensure that Health & Safety (H&S) requirements are fully complied with. (Repeat this exercise for all suppliers' details when their services have been confirmed.) Finally, at this stage, add any important dates relating to yourself and any key personnel working with you on the event. For example, if you have a two week holiday booked, add this information into the Schedule and be mindful to avoid these dates when assigning organisational duties.

Top Tip Tick:

If there is more than one person responsible for organising the event, this Benchmark Schedule is an excellent way of clarifying areas of responsibility – it helps to ensure that everyone is fully aware of the tasks assigned to them and of the agreed time frame by which action needs to have been undertaken.

So, there you go, this is the start of your Benchmark Schedule.

The next stage is to then look at your most up to date Event Costing and start at the top of the document. When considering the fictional event, see the first heading 'Invitation'… when scheduling organisational tasks on the Benchmark Schedule it truly is a matter of common sense most of the time. What is the point of prioritising the main organisation, if you leave it too late for guests to be able to accept an invitation – the first heading to sit firmly on your Schedule is, therefore, 'Invitations'.

Put your 'event organiser' hat firmly on and every time you place a heading into the Schedule try to think outside the box. So you place Invitation at the top of the list but try to think laterally, what else do you need to consider when contemplating invitations? Apart from the design and manufacture of a tangible invitation, you also need to consider the guest list, time frame and method of distribution. Then, if possible, assign the person responsible for each task and add this into the body of the Benchmark Schedule, detailing when the duty is to be undertaken and also apply the week when the duty has to be completed. When considering aspects such as RSVP dates, also take a moment to scan the details that you have input from the location. When does a location require final numbers? Take this particular deadline and any others into account allowing for some leeway.

Overleaf is an example Benchmark Schedule based on the fictional event. It includes those initial tasks that should be considered at this stage within the organisational process.

Happiness is a Ticked Off List!

Happiness is a Ticked Off List!

The Benchmark Schedule is a working document and should be amended accordingly and updated throughout the pre production phase - it is a very useful tool when trying to schedule your own and other people's workload. It is stressful enough organising an event let alone organising under crisis management conditions – so, when feasible, take note of important deadlines requested by all suppliers and work around these dates, ensuring that your organisation tasks are nicely spread throughout the period.

Top Tip Tick:

When updating the Action Status on your Benchmark Schedule, maintain the colour coding utilised on your Itinerary – this will help to identify, at a glance, the person responsible for finalising the task.

As the event develops, so will your Benchmark Schedule. When you feel that you have listed all the key organisational details known to date, take a look at the Ultimate Tick List (featured in Chapter 12) just to make certain that you have thought of everything that needs to be considered for the event you are organising and, if you have forgotten something, simply add it to the Benchmark Schedule as an action.

At the end of this book (Chapter 14) you will find a completed Benchmark Schedule, again, based on the fictional event. This will, hopefully, help you to complete your own Schedule based on the particular style event you are planning.

As mentioned previously, the Benchmark Schedule and the Itinerary should be utilised in conjunction with each other. Both documents will help to raise questions and, as such, for you to establish the answers and organise/plan accordingly. Standing alone they are each a powerful organisational tool but when utilised in unison, they are a force to be reckoned with.

Top Tip Tick:

When you have completed the first draft of your Benchmark Schedule, I would advise that this is forwarded to each person who has an active role in making the event happen. This will guarantee that everyone knows what is expected of them at any given time throughout the organisational process and time frame. I would also recommend regular progress meetings which will help to keep everyone on track whilst giving the opportunity to review the Benchmark timings and responsibilities accordingly. These progress meetings should feature within the Benchmark Schedule as shown on the example.

When you have formulated these two important documents, you can move on to the next phase of pre production, namely, the overall event design.

CHAPTER 3

Pre Production – Overall Event Design

Pre Production – Overall Event Design

Theme

There may be many reasons for an event taking place: a launch of a new product or internal motivational campaign, an anniversary, a thank you, an incentive... many, many reasons. Some of these functions require a theme even if it is just creating a new strap line for a conference. However, when considering this particular fictional event, the theming that I am talking about is definitely more along the conventional lines.

Take a look again at the Event Brief just to refresh your memory. When contemplating the fictional Event Brief, my eyes would be drawn towards the 'Event' i.e. party to celebrate the opening of an office in Paris and secondly, the 'Objective', that being to break away from tradition, with the emphasis being on fun.

So, in my mind, I would be looking to focus on both the 'Paris' and the 'fun' element and the best way to start building the overall event design which includes an element of theming, would be to revisit your Event Costing spreadsheet. You would need to consider how you could apply the overall theme to the various components of the event. With this fictional event in mind, try going through the associated spreadsheet headings, whilst considering the elements which could be themed.

You will notice that general 'theme' aspects have already been noted but the majority of the other elements, apart from the accommodation, could also facilitate a theme of some shape or form. For ease, let us divide the event into four distinct theming areas:

*   Pre Event
*   Pre Dinner Drinks
*   Dinner
*   Post Dinner

Top Tip Tick:

Once the location has been confirmed and your thoughts have turned towards the overall event design, time to schedule another site visit. Take a digital camera, pen, pad and tape measure to be on the safe side. When you arrive at the location you should be wearing your 'event organiser' hat. Walk through the event and the areas being utilised and take note of the location's colour scheme, carpets, chair colours etc. Take this opportunity to be shown the location's napery and crockery – anything which will help you to fully contemplate the event content and theme.

If you see a table that you anticipate using, an entrance or a door way or anything that you feel you may need to know the size of, take a moment to measure it and write down the measurements for later use. Take photos as well, this will all help in the long run.

One other important tip is to also wear your 'guest' hat (from the moment you walk into the location through to all areas being utilised) whilst considering the format of the event. Some locations are like rabbit warrens, calculate whether any directional signage would, therefore, be helpful and if it is so, work out how many left, right, up or downward directional arrows would be needed.

Also double check with the location what their policy is for erected signage and promotional material. Some don't allow signs to be affixed to a wall or signage to be erected in public areas. Either way, ask the location to confirm how many sign holders they have available along with their dimensions?

When you have contemplated the four distinct theming areas, this is where you need to also don your 'creative' hat and contemplate France, for a moment.

What do people wear, do, see, listen to?
What do people eat and drink?
How are people entertained?
What atmosphere and colour epitomises France/Paris?

Top Tip Tick:

I personally like to take some of my inspiration from my much thumbed reference books such as Cinema (which catalogues film releases and stories from 1894 – 2003) and also for general knowledge, I like to research utilising Chronicle of the 20th Century. In addition, books such as the World Travel Guide, provide valuable information on: climate, festivals, customs, temperature, locations, foods etc. There are many similar publications available right up to current day.

Of course, there is always the Internet. A wealth of knowledge can be sourced on many a good travel site.

If you can find a film or video that is based around your theme, then a lot of your research on colour, feel, clothing, music and food has already been done for you. Why reinvent the wheel!

NB: *Always ensure that the general feel of the event, including the entertainment, not only reflects the requirements of the host but also suits the type of guests attending.*

For this particular fictional event, my thoughts would be to combine various elements of Paris with the traditional and stereotypical flavour of generic France along with the fun & entertainment that is associated with the Moulin Rouge, the emphasis being on the *film* rather than the actual location.

Your next step would be, once this research has been undertaken, to consider how you can apply your thoughts and findings.

Let's look at the first of these four areas…

Pre Event

Teaser

A 'teaser' is either a fun, cryptic or classic communication which is sent to the invitee prior to the main invitation. If you are considering a theme for the event you are organising, this is the perfect way to charge the guest with anticipation. The objective is to ensure that the invitee is aware of the function and to place the date firmly in their diary in advance of receiving the actual invitation. A teaser can set the tone of the occasion and is especially important if the event is themed.

Teasers can be sent through the post utilising traditional print means or I find another effective method is to create an email teaser. Either way the wording or design can be the same.

Remember, it is not the formal invitation. It is just to *whet the appetite.*

Top Tip Tick:

If utilising a film to base the theme upon, it is always advisable to put a spin on the title just to avoid any copyright issues and be careful not to utilise any images which may also be copyright protected. It is always better to be safe than sorry.

Having read through reference books and watched the film, my thoughts on a teaser would be to create something like this…

Top Tip Tick:

Most people tend to send out invitations six weeks or so prior to the event. In this day and age where diaries are well and truly secured sometimes months in advance, I would recommend that an initial teaser or diary date be forwarded to the invitee between eight and twelve weeks in advance.

Invite

You may remember that part of this fictional brief was to endeavour to raise the bar as previous events had been, shall we say, mediocre. If you similarly need to break the mould, you are going to have to enhance expectations. Indeed, you are going to have to, at the outset, find a way to make the recipient identify that this event is going to be different from any previous functions that they have attended and is, therefore, a 'must go to' celebration.

You, or the person responsible, will have potentially already sent out an imaginative teaser so you are well on your way to changing perceptions but the best way to ensure that the invitee will be keen to confirm their attendance is to follow up with an attractive and once again, imaginative invitation.

Remember, the look and feel of an invite will set the tone of the whole event so great care and time should be taken over this vitally important aspect. If at all possible, make sure that the colours, images and type face utilised on a teaser follow through to the invitation and throughout the theming. The theming to include: menus, place cards and table plan, even the directional signs! This provides an effective, streamlined, well thought out effect.

Also, just as important is the *content* of an invitation. Remember, when I wrote earlier about receiving an invite and questioning what you looked for on the invite…Donning your 'guest' hat now, what information would you like to receive? When considering the fictional event, write down the details and then view the suggested information that I would feature.

Invite Content: *(based on the fictional event)*

To:	Mr Ken Bloggs and Miss Jane Smith *(guests name and partner's name, preferably personalised)*
From:	Mrs Lilly Smart, Chairwoman of Links Dearney Communications *(the host, his/her position and the host company)*
Branding:	Company logo *(if applicable)*
Reason:	To celebrate the opening of our new Paris office *(reason why the party is being held)*
Format:	Reception drinks, followed by dinner, entertainment and dancing *(detail what can be expected)*
Date:	Friday 24th July *(date)*
Time:	19.30 – Midnight *(timings)*
Dress Code:	Black tie or fitting for 'A Night at the Moulin Rouge' *(ensure clothing options are given where a theme is involved)*
Special Needs:	Please confirm any special dietary needs, allergies or disabilities you feel we should know about? *(important to get this feedback)*
RSVP:	June Weatherer by Fri 3rd July on 0207 444 5555 or june@linksdearney.com *(date to receive RSVPs and contact details – address to be added if required)*

Top Tip Tick:

When requesting notification on an invitation of 'any special needs', depending upon the type of function you are organising, one other request that should potentially be considered is whether the invitee has any 'phobias'. It sounds completely over the top, I know, but I found out the hard way when it came to light that one of the delegates attending an event that I organised had a phobia of butterflies. This would not normally have proved to be a problem but the hotel where the function was being held had a penchant for these insects. Butterfly pictures, butterfly sculptures, butterfly murals – you name it – butterflies everywhere. Bathrooms, hallways, bedrooms, meeting rooms. The situation was crisis managed on site and significant manpower was utilised in order to combat the butterfly threat – as they say, forearmed is forewarned!

Indeed, one of my clients told me of another situation where a guest transpired to have a phobia of 'sharing bedrooms' and 'loud noises'. This proved to be quite problematic as all guests were sharing twin rooms and the team activity was group drumming!

It will be your call to ask this somewhat unusual question – for this particular fictional event, I would not feel it to be truly appropriate.

To provide an example of how an invitation can be innovated to create a much desired buzz, the invitation overleaf shows a basic theme adaptation – if you have access to or the budget to commission a graphic designer then even better, the sky's the limit.

A personalised covering letter accompanying the invite can also clarify some other questions that the guests may have. When considering the fictional event, enclosing a map/directions whilst stating the car parking situation and positive transport links, would make it clear that the host is not providing transport. Clarifying that all pre-dinner drinks and wine with dinner will be provided with compliments, would hopefully guarantee that guests would bring some money for the bar after dinner. One other key form of clarification could be relating to the accommodation… stating that a special rate had been secured for all those guests who wish to stay overnight would also indicate that any booking and costs for overnight accommodation remains the responsibility of the guest.

A guest who has been provided with concise information will arrive in plenty of time, happy and relaxed – just the right frame of mind in which to help create that all important party spirit.

Mrs Lilly Smart, Chairwoman of Links Dearney Communications,
invites you to attend,

'come what may'

a celebration to commemorate the opening of the new Paris office

Friday 24th July

19.30   Reception Drinks
20.30   Dinner
22.00   Entertainment & Dancing
Midnight Carriages

Black tie or fitting for 'A night at the Moulin Rouge'

RSVP: June Weatherer by Fri 4th July

On: 0207 444 5555

Or   june@linksdearney.com

It's going to be a 'spectacular, spectacular' celebration!

Top Tip Tick:

Precise clarification is very important. All your hard work can be wasted should guests either assume or misinterpret the situation. To give you an example… I organised a VIP event overseas and the client's responsibility was to create and send out the invites along with a covering letter but for some reason or another the majority of the guests thought that they were going to be provided with clothing for the evening's gala reception. You can imagine the problems that this caused – fifty or so guests arriving in a different country with no shoes, frocks or tiaras! This meant that some key members of my event team had to be relieved of their scheduled duties to knock on the doors of clothing and shoe shops in order to organise rails of clothing and accessories to be delivered to the hotel. This put a great deal of pressure on the team, the client and of course the guests. Not to mention the financial implications. So always be clear and precise as to what you are, and in turn, are not providing.

So, you have considered the innovation of a teaser and invite, now is the time to continue your contemplation of the theming throughout the main three facets of this particular fictional event.

Pre Dinner Drinks

I personally like to 'build' a theme and an environment. I like guests to experience different things at different times which all add to the interest and enjoyment of the guests. When considering this fictional event, I am mindful that the budget is not unlimited so I feel that the best way to take this theme forward would be to focus on the generic Paris theme during the initial part of the evening (drinks reception) whilst progressing to Moulin Rouge for dinner and entertainment – after all, Moulin Rouge was famed for being a showcase for entertainment and of pure indulgence!

Drinks Reception

The first thing to do is to consider all the elements of a drinks reception…

- having a drink and bite to eat
- meeting other guests
- guests getting their bearings (toilets, cloakroom and checking out the table plan)
- providing the opportunity to relax and be entertained

I would contemplate the drink element first… is there anything special relating to France? Absolutely, Champagne! Now, not everyone likes Champagne so an option of a glass of French wine would also be welcomed by most guests. Do remember to serve a range of non-alcoholic drinks for those guests who do not wish to consume alcohol. Also, if providing a 'themed' drink, make sure that there is an alternative.

Top Tip Tick:

Although the focus of your theming should be on the basic formats/rooms utilised, don't forget the entrance way. Some locations will not allow a public entrance to be themed or personalised whilst others give carte blanche. Under these circumstances, take a moment to visualise how you could improve, personalise or theme such an area. Traditional adornments include red carpet, ropes and stands, personalised banners, flame burners and welcoming entertainers.

What about entertainment? Live music is always a good option but performers who play at a level to *encourage* discussion between the guests, rather than *competing* against, should be your preferred consideration. String quartets (classical and modern in style) are always enjoyed at a traditional evening affair; whilst entertainers in keeping with a theme such as a steel band for a Caribbean event can also help guests get into the spirit of the occasion.

However, for this particular fictional theme, how about providing a mime artiste to greet guests as they arrive and an accordionist and/or wandering violinist to provide the background music during the drink reception? Neither are too overwhelming when guests are mingling and wishing to talk to each other.

If budget is not available for live entertainment, do ensure that recorded music (in keeping with the theme) can be played in the background. You will need to establish with the location whether it has an independent sound system that is available in each of the areas utilised and if so, what format ie CD or, heaven forbid, tape. Alternatively, make sure that you source and provide your own equipment and material.

So music and entertainment sorted, how about nibbles? Canapés of course or why not snails as a delicacy? When considering the service of pre dinner nibbles, just raise the situation with the location on how it serves such items as canapés. Guests will soon identify the place where the staff appear with fresh salvers from the kitchen and the hungry guests may tend to hover around this area, quite often clearing the salver before the serving staff have had time to even enter the room which means those guests that are at the other side of the room sometimes miss out on pre dinner nibbles entirely, so best to just check on their circulation practice.

Top Tip Tick:

It is always a good idea to have some nibbles available for guests prior to a main dinner. It's not a good start if a guest is so hungry that he/she can't concentrate on enjoying the moment. With regard to the amount of pre dinner nibbles, this is normally driven by budget and the duration of the pre dinner drink period but a good rule of thumb is to choose between two – six canapés and allow for one or two 'bites/portions' per person of each. The more canapés you allow for, the more flexibility this gives to include both hot and cold canapés and meat/vegetarian options. Where canapés are concerned, variety is definitely the spice of life.

Also a word of advice – it is always worth spending a little bit extra on guaranteeing the quality of the beverages served during a drinks reception. Serving 'poor man's Champagne' is a false economy as, in my experience, guests tend to sip from their glass to be polite but leave their glasses half full when moving onto the next stage of the event.

Now that's the drink, the nibbles and the entertainment contemplated but what will guests see when they enter the reception area of our fictional event? When considering *generic* France for a moment, there is a wealth of theming that could be provided but it truly does depend upon the budget available. If budget and location allow, a Parisian street theme with props and a backdrop painted of the Paris skyline could be created or, if a more conservative budget is available as in our fictional event, it's amazing the transformation that colourful floor mounted, helium filled, balloons of red, white and blue could make. Combine this with striking material swags and patriotic flags, along with some white crisp table cloths and single red roses adorning the occasional tables and/or a magnificent pedestal arrangement incorporating the invitation – these theming elements could provide the perfect setting for a drinks reception.

Top Tip tick:

When considering the theming, you may have had to return many times to the location to contemplate your theming design. Take into account the hotel or venue's fixtures and fittings. Complement not detract from these. For example, if wanting to utilise orange as a colour but the carpet is bright pink you may need to reconsider. As mentioned previously, always ask to see the location's crockery and enquire about colour schemes of its napery – it is essential that you work together, this way the event will look seamless and fantastic.

Drinks to Dinner

Consider for a moment how you would move the fictional guests from one internal place to another. Could you theme this seemingly innocuous task to add a little showmanship to the occasion? Instead of asking the Banqueting Manager to simply make an announcement, how about a flamboyant 'master of ceremonies' similar to the character in the film, Mr Harold Zidler, welcoming guests *to the show* and inviting them to join him at the Links Dearney's very own Moulin Rouge?

I also mentioned previously that I like to lead guests through a multitude of experiences. Call upon your creativity and, if budget allows, think how you could transform the entrance into the dining location. In this instance, it could be by utilising a simple red carpet or you could elaborate and create, again by props and painted backdrop, the doorway to the Moulin Rouge. As an alternative, a red swish curtain could be erected for guests to walk through, with jugglers and fire eaters lining the route thereby building the anticipation of the guests.

Just prior to the guests entering the dining location, contemplate for a moment the table plan. Do you just want to create a traditional table plan or provide a table plan with a twist? The table numbers could be in French i.e. Table Une or each table could be named after a famous French city or a French wine. In this fictional scenario, as we are loosely basing the theme on Moulin Rouge, then you could name the tables as aspects from the film such as The Sparkling Diamond, Green Fairy, Diamond Dogs and King of Nightime Pleasures – tweaked to avoid any copyright issues. You get the picture…table plans and table numbers can always be enhanced to reflect a theme, whatever the theme may be.

Talking of table plans, I always recommend at least two types are produced and displayed. The first being an alphabetical list which simply states the name of the guest followed by their table number/description. Then the second lists the order of the number of tables and details the guests sitting at each table. (There is a third option and that is an actual floor plan specifying where the tables are placed within the room. This is very helpful for location staff as guests with special dietary needs can be identified for ease and efficiency.)

When considering the table plans always make sure that there are two sets. For this particular fictional event, one set should be placed in table plan holders at the drinks reception area whilst the other should be placed close to the entrance of the dining location – it's amazing how many guests forget where they are sitting in-between walking from the drinks reception to dinner.

Top Tip Tick:

Once an RSVP guest list has been collated, this should be forwarded to the person responsible for creating the individual place cards. If having names of guests calligraphied, this can take some considerable time so best to forward the list as soon as possible to allow the calligrapher to get to work. It is always easier to amend or replace a few names at the eleventh hour rather than create the entire guest list.

(Always remember, nevertheless, to take some spare place cards and a nice pen on site as there will undoubtedly be last minute name changes.)

Dinner

As guests leave one area and enter into another, what you should be aiming to do is create a 'wow' factor. The room should look stunning and there are some simple ways to achieve this without having to break the bank.

When considering this particular theme, I would focus on the 'love' aspect of the film – which firstly relates to the host company 'loving' France so much so that they decided to open an office in this exuberant city, and secondly, for providing the perfect opportunity to create a sumptuous setting for the dining and entertainment experience. As the fictional guests move into the dining room, I would wish them to enter into a plush environment with wonderful depth created by the use of deep, passionate red as the dominant colour. Heart shaped red balloons and gold swags could adorn the room whilst smoke could fill the floor with rays of light framing the dance floor thereby creating a night club/dance hall feel.

Top Tip Tick:

If providing table arrangements with candles, you will need to have checked previously if the location allows naked flame and, if they do, be mindful if having paper napkins, crackers or party poppers as these can smoulder rather easily - just pay attention during the dinner to help avoid any mini table fires.

Themed table arrangements incorporating a top hat, fresh red roses, 'diamonds' and candle light would look stunning in this setting - you should never under estimate the effect of a gorgeous table setting.

If at all possible, make sure that cups refrain from being placed on the tables prior to coffee time as this will cramp the tables and a cup free environment guarantees that there will be plenty of space available to display a wonderful table centre such as the one described. Gone are the days when table centres were over-flowery and twee, now they can be striking and unique – wherever possible ensure that table arrangements include candles as this helps to create a magical environment.

If budget allows, how about adding some glamour to the chairs by hiring some bold chair covers and/or coloured table linen plus some eye catching charger plates and red glass water goblets. Providing some adornments for the guests such as red feather boas for the ladies and top hats for the gents would be fun and very much in keeping when taking this fictional event into account.

Top Tip Tick:

Take some time prior to the event to contemplate the music throughout. Although it is always preferable to link music to a theme, especially initially, do bear in mind that dinner on average takes approximately one and a half hours to consume and guests may get a little fed up hearing a film soundtrack for the umpteenth time! My suggestion would be to start with themed and then generalise the music and make sure that you have purchased any specific CDs that are needed well in advance. Of course, if you have a good budget, a full blown orchestra would suit this particular theme very well indeed. If not, CDs would be perfectly acceptable.

Menu

There are two aspects you could consider when applying a theme – provide a menu, in this case French, or provide English cuisine but with names fitting the theme.

Menu selection is always a difficult aspect of event organising. It is normally best for the brief provider to select a menu as they will undoubtedly know their guests and be best placed to make this decision. Rule of thumb… stay away from game or too complicated food. Guests have happily been eating beef on a regular basis for some time now, lamb (when in season) is very popular whilst pork is also well received by the majority and of course the good old favourite, chicken is still very popular and tends to be less costly than the other meats. Fish, nevertheless, tends to be selected as a vegetarian option or as a starter.

These days many guests do have allergies whilst some have religious requirements and moral grounds when selecting their menus. I mentioned that guests should be asked to confirm any special dietary needs and these should be notified to the location hosting the event well in advance.

When you are provided with details of the guests' special dietary needs, don't be surprised if two types of vegetarian attend i.e. a 'vegetarian' who eats fish and a vegetarian who is strict and avoids fish – you may need to try to arrange for two vegetarian options for the main course or plump for serving one dish which does not contain fish.

Regardless of the number of vegetarians you have allowed for, also be aware that additional vegetarians may very well appear overnight! The previous day, they were meat eaters and then the next, totally vegetarian. This normally arises when guests see an appetising vegetarian dish whilst sitting at their dining table and decide they fancy that dish instead of the one they are being served – chefs tend to allow for this in their calculations, irritating though it might be.

Top Tip Tick:

Spare more than a passing thought for the vegetarians. I generally feel that vegetarians at corporate functions can get the raw end of the deal. Even the most easy going vegetarian must get fed up with a Medley of Stir Fried Vegetables or Mushroom Stroganoff. Talk to the chef and if you are not happy with the vegetarian suggestions, discuss at length and see how the options can be created to be a little more imaginative.

For large numbers of guests just one menu will need to be selected. (Plus a vegetarian option.) Many locations will only allow a set menu to be served although some will allow two starters and two main dishes to be chosen on the night – it is best to clarify the location's policy on menu choice at the outset.

Depending upon the number of guests attending, you may be directed to select a cold starter. Regardless of whether a hot or a cold starter is chosen, always ensure that the dish is only served when you wish the guests to start eating. If a guest sits down and their starter is already on the table, you cannot blame them if they decide to tuck in! This can cause many a problem should there be a welcome speech scheduled before the meal is due to commence. Nothing can be more off putting for someone speaking to the gathering if some guests are busy eating. Also, these guests will then have to sit and wait some considerable time whilst others consume their starter after any welcoming speeches and before the main course is served. So remember that starters are only to be placed on the table at the time when guests are to be encouraged to commence their dining experience.

I always feel that it is the quality of the food and the presentation that wins hands down every time. If you or the brief provider feels that the guests are likely to be adventurous and you are confident that the chef at the location can provide, say, for this fictional event, a truly French fayre, then why not suggest going for it? If your gut feeling is to play it a little safer, then suggest opting for more traditional dishes but creating some fun themed names and arrange for some menu cards to be printed. Themed names such as these:

Gothic Tower
Timbale of Prawns, Avocado and Papaya

Duke's Delight
Supreme of Chicken on a bed of Gourmet Mushrooms & Shallots
Served with an apple laced rosti and fresh Garden Vegetables

L'Amour, L'Amour
Banoffee Pie

Top Tip Tick:

Hotel and venue's caterers can arrange for a menu tasting prior to confirmation of the menu and wine selection. Depending upon the size of the event, some charge for this service whilst others don't. If you are unsure of the menu choice or just wish to feel confident that the food is going to be as good as desired, it is always worthwhile to arrange a tasting.

Formats of menu tasting are also different for each catering establishment. As a rule of thumb, you and your boss, colleague or client can select the full anticipated menu choice or up to two/three starters/main courses plus vegetarian options and dessert dishes. A red and a white wine can also normally be tasted at the same time. You will not be expected to sit down and eat full plates of food; you will just sample each dish and select your favourite.

> *NB: Some, but not all, may also allow you to sample any canapés being considered.*

Wine

These days every location provides a good wine selection and even house wines are normally more than palatable. On this occasion, the wine and indeed water, if having bottled, simply has to be French. If budget allows, how about, when considering a digestif, that some French brandy or, dare I say, some Absinthe is offered?

Taking into account the importance of a perfectly set dining table, it is best to identify with the location how it will be serving the wine, whatever the choice. Most four/five star locations will automatically serve wine whilst some locations will place a bottle of red and a bottle of white (in a cooler) on the table for guests to help themselves.

The latter is not the preferred method of service as it does tend to clutter the table and lessen the overall experience, so if possible, have the wine poured but ensure that you are aware of any costing ramifications should additional staff be needed to provide this service, especially for larger number of guests.

There is one alternative option to serving the location's wine and that is to consider suggesting to your boss, colleague or client to bring their own! Some people prefer to do this but be prepared for a hefty 'corkage' charge. Corkage charges vary from location to location but if this option is required, you will need to arrange with the location for 'chilling' and 'storing' so make sure that all beverages arrive well in advance of the event.

Adornments

That's the food and the wine sorted – what about the serving staff? Some locations are game to play their part and are willing for their staff to wear clothing to suit the occasion as long as it doesn't interfere with the provision of their service.

For example, getting a waitress to serve Champagne in a big elephant suit is not likely to be warmly received (it's not likely to happen anyway but you know what I mean) but asking serving staff to wear French aprons for a theme of this particular nature, would normally be more than acceptable.

Do bear in mind the consequential costs incurred for the hiring and potential cleaning of any specific clothing that you wish the location's staff to wear.

Entertainment

There are many forms of entertainment when contemplating themes of a country origin.

If you feel that the event would benefit from some entertainment during dinner, close hand magicians are a good golden oldie - they never fail to impress and positively entertain guests whilst remaining unobtrusive. If you would like an entertainer to tailor him or herself to a theme then he/she should normally be able to oblige. A close hand magician could easily be modified to a French theme of this nature, for instance; by dressing as a person frequenting the Moulin Rouge. He or she could personalise tricks by making a Euro, 'diamond' or rose magically appear from behind someone's ear, rather than the traditional pound coin. Indeed, instead of making an everyday bottle of wine magically traverse through a table, a bottle of Champagne could be considered – you never know he/she may even be up for performing with a French accent!

However, for this particular theme a caricaturist with the drawing style or costume of Toulouse Lautrec would be perfect. Guests always like to see a caricature of themselves and it does provide such a lasting memento of the occasion. In between courses allows for additional entertainment and one that would be fitting and exhilarating to watch would be a Tango performed by two professional dancers to the Roxanne track as featured in the film.

Should you require entertainers that do not perform at tables per se but where guests are sitting down, such as a band, do remember that you may need to factor in the requirement for a raised stage area. In addition, you may also like to arrange a backdrop to frame the entertainers who are performing on stage. Some locations will possess their own stage environment and will provide this free of charge, likewise, the same goes for a dance floor. Do be warned, nonetheless, many locations charge extra for both.

When considering where the entertainers will perform, thought must also be given to the lighting. Again some locations will have in house equipment for such requirements or they will probably be able to recommend a supplier to provide lighting for the stage and also, if budget allows, to light the dance floor which helps to create a more 'dance' friendly environment. Do ensure that any costs for lights, stage, back drop, dance floor and/or sound are allocated for within your overall event costing.

For this particular theme, creating a back drop replicating the red heavy drape curtains would be perfect, or a projection/structure of the famous 'windmill' onto a plain backdrop would be equally impressive.

Top Tip Tick:

Some event requirements will call for the actual walls to be dressed and one of the most effective ways is to erect star cloth curtain. Although very impressive (star cloth curtain is black cloth incorporating small lights that can twinkle and change colour) utilising a significant amount of material can increase the temperature within the room dramatically. Bear this in mind and only contemplate this form of theming should the location have good air conditioning.

Post Dinner

Straight after dinner/coffee can be the time to up the ante. The best way to do this, in my opinion, is to provide some great entertainment and, if the guests' profiles suit, to kick start the after dinner entertainment with some audience participation.

A fabulous form of entertainment for this particular theme would be some traditional Can Can girls which is perfect for incorporating audience participation overseen by the flamboyant 'master of ceremonies'. For alternative forms of participative entertainment of a different theme you could select salsa or ballroom dancing or the like. Participative entertainment is great fun to do and watch, and a sure way to arouse the senses after guests have been sitting down for some time.

When guests have had a giggle, normally at their colleagues' expense, now is the time to provide some generic entertainment. Again, try to link the after dinner entertainment to the theme and for this fictional event a band playing all the songs featured in the film would be great. The evening could then progress by means of a more traditional disco just to make certain that there is something for everyone to enjoy.

But what about those guests who do not want to dance? A fun casino, in this case named the Montmartre

Casino although perfect for a French theme can lend itself to many other themes and is as popular today as it was many years ago. Thus, the French twist could be that the personalised money be produced in Euros rather than the usual *dollars* and feature an icon of the Moulin Rouge windmill whilst incorporating the Links Dearney Communications logo.

NB: For some additional entertainment ideas suited to alternative themes and events, I have incorporated the most popular within the Ultimate Tick List featured in Chapter 12.

I have mentioned that the theme should run throughout the event, so don't forget the prizes. If having a raffle, or indeed, wish to award the person who has won the most chips playing on the fun casino tables, prizes fitting to the fictional event could include: a weekend trip to Paris and of course two tickets to the Moulin Rouge, a meal for two in a fantastic French restaurant, roses for a year, CDs, diamond earrings, dancing lessons, picnic hamper, Champagne and French wine. The list is quite literally endless.

Finally, I always like to end an event with a flourish, what about you? Confetti cannons or a balloon drop are a fabulous way to close an event with finality yet leaving guests on a high and in this case, red and white confetti did, indeed, feature at the conclusion of the film, so what a great way to signify The End.

Top Tip Tick:

Securing a quality photographer to capture moments of the event can be worth its weight in gold. If the budget does not stretch, make sure that someone is specifically tasked to take photographs throughout the function – as an event manager, this will, understandably, not be one of your priorities and so classic moments will undoubtedly be lost but it is better than nothing.

That's the ticket and, hopefully, although these theming examples are far from exhaustive, you will understand the process you can follow in order to develop *any* theme for *any* type of event. The theming should begin from the very first form of communication all the way through to the end of the event and I always feel that theming is limited by budget rather than imagination...

When your thought process is complete, I would advise that you list on a simple word document, all the theming ideas that you have contemplated against each section of the event i.e. in this case: pre event, pre dinner drinks, dinner and post dinner. Don't worry if they are not in exact event schedule order, just something like this:

Pre Event:
Teaser
Invite (design and print)

Happiness is a Ticked Off List!

Misc:
Photographer

Pre Dinner Drinks:
Improvement of entrance way: red carpet, ropes, banners, flame burner
Champagne drinks reception
Entertainer – accordionist & violinist
Entertainer – mime artiste
Music – background CD
Canapés
Parisian street theme (props and backdrops)
Helium balloons
Swags and flags

Dinner:
Master of Ceremonies
MC's costume
Red carpet
Props and painted backdrop (Moulin Rouge entrance)
Red swish curtain (entrance to Moulin Rouge and/or backdrop to stage)
Entertainer – juggler
Entertainer – fire-eater
Themed table plan (print out)
Themed table descriptions (numbers)
Place cards
Room theming:
Red heart balloons (floor mounted)
Red heart balloons (table top)
Red and gold swags
Smoke
Atmospheric lighting
Themed table arrangements
Chair covers
Table linen, charger plates and red water goblets
Gifts – red feather boas
Gifts – top hats
Music – film/soundtrack
Music – misc CDs
Music - orchestra
Dinner menu

Menu card
Wine
Waiters clothing (French aprons)
Entertainment – caricaturist
Entertainment – Tango performance
Windmill
Stage, lighting and sound
Dance floor

Post Dinner:
Digestif (Brandy or Absinthe)
Entertainment – Can Can dancers
Entertainment – band
Entertainment – disco
Entertainment – fun casino
Prizes
Confetti cannon
Balloon drop

There you have it, a complete list of your theming ideas.

Event Content and Suppliers

Having now fully contemplated your theme ideas, by utilising the theming list, your next step would be to locate suitable suppliers to fulfil the theming needs. This will then enable you to incorporate accurate costs into your Event Costing, thereby clarifying the exact theming elements you can afford to propose within budget.

Top Tip Tick:

When creating your theming list, be mindful of the budget that you have allocated for theming elements. It is extremely time consuming sourcing suppliers and establishing costings so if only able to set aside a conservative amount of money but your theming ideas quite clearly indicate a larger budget may well be needed, utilise your time wisely by prioritising and establish the costs first for those elements of theming that you feel would probably be able to be included in the budget. If, after calculating overall costs, there is some money spare then you can embark on further investigation to establish costs of those theming ideas placed on the Optional Extra list.

Happiness is a Ticked Off List!

There are many ways in which to source suppliers.

* Internet
* Trade publications
* Exhibitions
* Specialist companies/agents
* Recommendation

Similar to researching a location, there are comparable options available when considering event content by utilising both the Internet (including sourcing associations) and trade publications such as the comprehensive CES along with magazines (distributed upon application) which feature reports on aspects such as locations, entertainers and general suppliers such as Event and M&it.

There are also a number of exhibitions specially created for the events industry. Some, similar to the venue exhibitions, restrict the attendees to 'trade' whilst others welcome people who are responsible for organising events regardless of their true nature of business. 'RSVP' is one such exhibition. Also there are agents such as Peter Johnson and Sternberg Clarke who promote and act as agents for various suppliers such as; caricaturists, close hand magicians, themers, bands, and opera performers among others.

Top Tip Tick:

As a matter of course, I would recommend that a copy of a reputable agency's representation brochure or catalogue is obtained as you can use this as a reference tool to provide ideas and guideline prices from many suppliers for a range of different events.

Hopefully, a location has been chosen that you are comfortable with, which mirrors your and the brief provider's desired quality and ethos. If this is the case, it's always a good idea to ask the location if they can recommend any suppliers - they may possess a list of preferred suppliers. This way, I personally believe that the location has a *moral* obligation to ensure that the supplier they recommend is of a certain standard and reliability.

Finally, good old 'word of mouth'. Ask your colleagues and friends – I am sure that they will be more than happy to share good contacts with you.

Regardless of how you locate potential suppliers, it is always advisable to ask for references and to ensure that you religiously take these up and undertake the credential checks.

Top Tip Tick:

All suppliers should have adequate Public Liability insurance. As a rule of thumb anything between £2m - £5m, depending upon the risk level of the service the supplier will be providing, should be the range of cover you should be looking for.

In addition, and in accordance with Health & Safety Law (H&S), most suppliers should be able to provide Risk Assessments. (See Chapter 7 for further details.)

Securing Suppliers

When you have identified a potential supplier, you will need to contact them to ascertain their availability. If they are available, you will need to provide an outline of your requirements, ask for a quote in writing (along with a copy of their terms and conditions) and seek confirmation that they do indeed have adequate insurance coverage along with any relevant Risk Assessment documents.

NB: You may like to also consider asking some key suppliers if they have a Business Continuity Plan (BCP) in place prior to confirming their services. A supplier's BCP basically outlines their process for when things unexpectedly go wrong prior to the event taking place. For example, what would happen if a selected Production Company had a fire and all their equipment was damaged or indeed all the master footage went up in flames? Would they have emergency suppliers they could draw upon and would they have backed up software kept safely off site? Knowing of the contingencies in place, especially with key suppliers who could make or break the success of an event, would ultimately provide that extra peace of mind.

This may also be a good time to establish whether they also have any sustainability measures in place, however limited they may be.

When you have received all the required quotes, amend 'allocations' with accurate costs into your Event Costing which should already feature the accurate quote from the selected location, including: costs for main room hire, menu and drinks prices etc. Your accurate costing document for this fictional event, which is a development of the original event costing spreadsheet (headings being more specific and placed into the four key areas of the event) may now look like this:

(You will notice that the Contingency content now lists some logistical elements which will be considered during the 'logistical' process as described in Chapter 4.)

Happiness is a Ticked Off List!

Top Tip Tick:

When considering caterers, you may not automatically think of them as a supplier, especially if a hotel has been selected as the location. Therefore, should a venue be chosen which determines the need to secure a catering company, do choose carefully. Some caterers charge one price per head for providing the menu whilst others charge elements separately such as: menu, staffing, catering equipment, delivery/washup and collection. When totalled, this can prove to be a costly option, so my advice is to clarify their method of charging at the outset and when comparing prices, ensure that all costs are known so that a like for like comparison can be undertaken.

Even when incorporating just the theming ideas that were of preference, it transpired that I was initially a little over the fictional budget. However, you may be in the fortunate situation one day to be able to incorporate all your ideas and that would be absolutely fabulous.

So, should you find yourself in a similar situation, this is where you have to go back to the costing (see example) and only retain those elements that are an absolute necessity to the event and place any surplus theming ideas at the bottom of the spreadsheet along with the other aspects already listed under 'Optional Extras'. This may take you a little time to do but your objective is to bring the event in within budget.

I should point out that, although at this stage you are developing a more accurate costing, it will never be completely accurate until you have fully developed the event and considered the 'logistics'. Consequently, still maintaining a healthy Contingency is strongly recommended until all elements of the event can be contemplated. Only when all the steps have been undertaken will you be able to produce an absolutely accurate Event Costing but you will be well on your way at this stage.

Top Tip Tick:

If you find that you are close but not quite within budget but you especially wish for a particular element of theming – you can always go back to the supplier and ask if there are any circumstances that they would negotiate on their quote. You never know, it could make all the difference.

After you have undertaken the task of creating an event on budget, this is the ideal time to meet with the brief provider to discuss your theming ideas in detail – they may be able to find some additional budget to incorporate some extra theming from the Optional Extras list. Your objective at this meeting is to gain authority to proceed with specific theming so that you can firm up suppliers.

Top Tip Tick:

Although not specifically aimed at 'theming' suggestions, if you have recommended an element that you feel is crucial to the successful organisation and management of the event but the brief provider decides not to follow your advice, do make it clear that you can't take responsibility for the outcome of this decision. To give you an example of this situation…I once had a client who wished my company to organise an outdoor concert for them. They did not have the budget to utilise our first choice production company so a secondary 'cheaper' supplier was established. This supplier's equipment was not as premier as the preferred company's but regardless, they recommended a certain sized sound system which took into account key aspects such as: the dimensions of the stage, type of bands playing (and of their requirements), area of land being utilised for the concert and the number of guests attending but the clients thought that this recommendation was excessive and requested the sound system to be reduced in size in order to save some money.

This cost cutting exercise proved to be detrimental to the event as unfortunately, although the importance of quality sound was again stressed, by actioning their directive, the sound just wasn't powerful or the quality clear enough for the audience coverage. All being well, your boss, colleague or client will, however, readily accept all your recommendations whether these be related to theming ideas or practicalities of the event.

When you have gained authority to proceed with your theming ideas and you are happy with the suppliers that you have sourced, if relevant, ask to meet them face to face prior to any formal confirmations being made. If they are a band, ask them to provide a photograph, a demo of their work or better still establish where they are playing so that you can see them perform prior to securing their services. Talk, ask for examples of their work – thorough research is what it is all about and the more time you can give to this aspect the better.

After you have undertaken the leg work and wish to proceed with a specific supplier(s), with the brief provider's blessing, the next step would be to send a letter of confirmation. For an 'entertainer' you may like to include the following key details in your confirmation, similar details to be tailored to suit alternative suppliers.

- Requested time of performance
- Location (address, website and map)
- Their required dress code
- The duration of the performance
- The agreed fee and when this will be paid
- Whether providing subsistence/accommodation
- Set up and load out times

Also, don't forget to ask each supplier if they have any special dietary requirements, their approximate arrival time and their mobile contact numbers in case you need to speak to them when they are en route to the event. Always, always confirm your requirement to suppliers in writing.

Depending upon the type of supplier you are confirming, you may or may not subsequently receive a contract from them which should replicate your confirmation details.

Top Tip Tick:

One final aspect you may wish to consider is how you would like the suppliers to be perceived — if you don't want them to readily be promoting their services and handing out their business cards at the event, then simply tell them.

So, when you have firmed up all the suppliers, on to the next step.

CHAPTER 4

Pre Production – Concluding Organisation

Pre Production – Concluding Organisation

Since embarking on the journey to become a proficient event organiser, you should now be party to the vital steps and the order in which you need to take them.

So let's recap:

- You have learned how to take and create an Event Brief.
- You have leaned how to source locations and create a Location Brief.
- You have learned how to apply good administrative housekeeping techniques.
- You have learned how to create an Event Costing.
- You have learned how to identify, liaise and confirm a suitable location.
- You have learned how to create the, all important, Event Itinerary.
- You have learned how to create the, equally important, Benchmark Schedule.
- You have learned how to consider the concept and design of an event.
- You have learned how to locate and confirm suitable suppliers.
- Most importantly, you are learning how to 'think' like a proficient event organiser.

I cannot emphasise enough how important it is to keep your files well managed and to keep on top of the tasks featured on your To Do List. In particular, at the beginning of each week, check on your Benchmark Schedule to clarify exactly what needs to be achieved during the course of that particular period and clearly state when a task has been actioned. Continue to ask questions and to add them into your Event Itinerary - strive every day to convert questions into statements. You will soon see how the event is building and naturally more and more questions will materialize.

Top Tip Tick:

Although for emergencies you can utilise your Extra Cost Sheet, I would suggest that whenever there is an amendment which has a ramification upon the event costing, you immediately make the amendment on your spreadsheet. This means that by the time the event is pretty much organised, your costing will be bang up to date and so when the day comes to finalise costs and check against final supplier invoices, it won't be such a mammoth task.

Logistics

Logistics are normally considered at the latter part of the organisational phase. This is because the logistical process can only be undertaken after all the key elements have been organised and their details incorporated into an itinerary. Key information such as the arrival and departure times of guests and suppliers, along with the clarification of the complete event format and details of all inclusions are crucial.

So 'visualisation' is needed once again. When reading through your Itinerary, put your 'guest' hat back on whilst wearing jauntily to the side your 'event organiser' hat and commence the concluding organisational process.

Let's start with the 'guest' hat and let us assume that you are one of the guests attending this fictional event and you have decided to drive. You have been sent full directions and arrive with ease at the hotel and you are pleased to see that there are indeed plenty of car parking spaces. You park and walk to the entrance. Now ask yourself some searching questions. Where do I go? You see a directional sign which you instantly recognise as the stylization is similar to the invite…You follow the signs which direct you, as a guest, through to a private drinks reception area where it will be obvious where to leave your coat and that you are looking forward to being offered a complimentary drink.

Now contemplating this very initial part of a guest's experience and wearing your 'event organiser' hat, consider each element that needs to be managed on site.

So let's look at each step of the guest's experience. No problems with the invite as they will have been designed either in house or out sourced and consideration will have been given regarding the details that need to feature on the invite along with the helpful information incorporated into the covering letter. You will have contemplated who was going to action the creation of the invites, the invitee list, the physical addressing of the envelopes along with the posting and all will have been planned well in advance of any key deadlines – so, in short, everything is rosy and a good turnout is very much anticipated.

When the guest arrives at the hotel, he/she sees the directional signs and that's great because, like the invites, you will have already actioned these. But question one thing, how were the directional signs erected? You will now need to build into your Itinerary a personnel logistic and that is to schedule the erection of the directional signs. Take this one step further, what will this person need in order to erect the directional signs? I.e. directional sign holders or White Tac, should this be allowed. Write a question into the Itinerary, have you got White Tac? Do you have to buy any to place into your Tool Box? (See Chapter 11.) Then contemplate that, although the guests will see directional signs, it would be a nice touch to also be personally greeted. Have you allocated a person to undertake this role? If not, add it to the Itinerary.

When guests enter the reception area, who is managing the cloakroom – have you organised for this to be operated by the location staff? Write it into your Itinerary to contemplate how many coats may need to be stowed and ask the hotel how much they charge? Arrange for adequate location personnel. Finally, when guests have deposited their coats, time for a drink. Contemplate the position of the cloakroom and where guests will be served their drinks. Have you clarified to the hotel the location of where the drinks should be served? It's no good having the drinks set up in a place that is prior to the cloakroom – as you don't want guests trying to remove their coats whilst clutching a glass, very clumsy. Have you confirmed with the hotel that you want tray service? Add all these questions into your Itinerary.

When you have gone through the whole format of the event and calculated the personnel logistics, then you can finalise how many management staff are needed for the event and organise accordingly. You will also be able to establish transportation requirements/details for any event manager and of their desired arrival time.

Top Tip Tick:

When considering logistics on site you will need to communicate on a regular basis with any event management team. The best way to do this is with two way walkie-talkies (radios) and covert earpieces. This will save so much time and effort as you can speak freely to each other, even if one of you is on the top floor and the other is on the ground floor. Covert earpieces are essential for keeping disruption to the minimum.

You can hire or buy two way radios – I always find that it is much easier to hire them on a daily or weekly basis from a supplier as they have all the necessary licenses. You should easily be able to find one within your area. (Do make sure that you also secure spare batteries, holsters and chargers and you double check if there are any particular channels that you need to utilise for the particular handsets hired.)

Event Managers

You may like to consider hiring professional event managers from a reputable freelance agency or the brief provider may wish you to head up the event management side with the help of some of your work mates. When considering the event personnel, they need to be: trustworthy, hard working, have a great deal of stamina, a good sense of humour, a *share and share alike* work ethic and of course be presentable. Either way, it is important that their services are formally confirmed so they know exactly what is expected of them.

Top Tip Tick:

As a rule of thumb the ratio for event management to guests are 1:50 but it truly does depend upon the format of the event and making sure that enough personnel are available to undertake all the logistical duties - I always try to ensure that there are at least two event personnel on duty regardless of the number of guests attending. Never under estimate how many people it will take to carry out a seemingly simple task, like moving guests from one room to another.

In particular, you should confirm details such as the: date, location, duties, timings, dress code and expenses along with payment and payment terms (if applicable). You should also ask the event manager(s) to formally confirm that they are happy to accept the role as detailed, seek confirmation they will help to improve sustainable performance and abide by H&S as directed (as explained in Chapter 7) and keep confidential any information they are exposed to whilst at the same time request confirmation of their mobile telephone number.

Depending upon the source of the event management team, you may wish to confirm their employment status i.e. self employed or employed. In addition, you may wish to confirm whether they have their own Public Liability insurance cover or whether you will need to arrange for them to come under the policy covering the company that you are working on behalf of or your own cover should you be in the position to have the need for insurance.

Top Tip Tick:

When considering the clarification of dress code, if securing event managers to help with the running of outdoor events – don't forget to either provide wet weather and warm clothing or ask the event manager to provide their own should you be happy with 'non uniform' clothing.

When it comes to internal events, likewise, it is best to specify what you, or the brief provider, would like the event team to wear or to provide clothing appropriate to the nature of the event should it be wished for everyone to be uniformly dressed.

Generally, when considering dress code, anticipate what the duties are likely to be throughout the event. I always prefer to wear clothes that allow for my radio to be discreet. I tend to wear trousers of some sort with shoes that have a lowish heel so that I can undertake tasks such as climbing on stage without losing my dignity! Think practical – you are there to work, not to be one of the glamorous guests.

One final tip: During the setting up period – trainers are a must. Comfy shoes and heels are to be saved for the event itself. Take care of your feet, you will need all their support later.

One aspect that many forget to organise is the use of 'space'. When contemplating the logistics also think about what you as an event manager are going to need and to do. For example if you or a member of the event team are responsible for compiling delegate badging, you are going to need a private space to do this as you can't spill out over public areas of a location. If you are going to need a production meeting with the event team, where will this take place? What about your lap top, do you need to set this up? I previously mentioned using a production office but what about suppliers, do they need changing room facilities? Does anyone need to store boxes or clothing etc? What about the florist, does she/he need a cool room with ready access to water? Contemplate all these requirements and then organise additional function rooms if needed.

You will find, by undertaking this exercise, you will create a great number of further questions and dilemmas that need to be fully considered but it does mean that once you have visualised the whole event, then you will have hopefully covered the entire logistics and also ensured the right number of event management personnel have been secured to proficiently manage the event.

Subsistence and Accommodation

Remember to factor in food and drink for all event managers, crew and on site personnel (including suppliers if applicable) for the duration that they are present at the location – this includes loading in, set up and load out periods. Make sure that you have established the number of personnel on site and if anyone, like the guests, has a special dietary need, take this into account when organising subsistence. It is vital that all those personnel working on the event are properly fed and watered; everyone needs to keep their strength up and so, wherever possible, build in adequate breaks. (In addition to finding space for changing and storage you may also need to contemplate the need for a subsistence room, or to save an uncomfortable situation, subsistence room(s) should the level of subsistence vary between the suppliers and the crew/event management.)

Finally, when contemplating timings and the distance of the location, you may need to consider accommodation for on site personnel. Most in house personnel and event managers are prepared to share rooms whilst crew, suppliers and senior management tend only to be happy in single occupancy rooms. If accommodation is required, make sure that you obtain numbers and details in order to finalise the accommodation requirements and provide a rooming list to the location.

The accommodation doesn't have to be at the same location as the event, but out of preference, I would always advise it thus. Always make it clear if you wish these guests to be responsible for settling their own room extras upon departure and doubly ensure that the location is aware of this arrangement.

You need to obviously ensure that both the subsistence and accommodation elements have been factored into your overall costing. Either way, it may be cheaper to pay separately for refreshments, lunch, dinner and B&B on a special 'crew' rate or it may be less expensive to secure a 24 hour delegate rate.

Hopefully, you will see what is involved with this final stage. As I said before, it is all about PLANNING, PLANNING and more PLANNING.

Working hand in hand with logistics is the understanding of how you can do your bit to reduce the carbon footprint of the event. Hopefully, you will have already undertaken your own measures throughout the pre production phase but what of the event day itself? When undertaking the visualization process, don another hat, your 'environment' hat and work through the event, whilst taking into account the location and supplier measures that they already have in place, contemplate any additional measures that you could implement. For example…if creating delegate packs, try to use recycled paper and format them to minimise the amount of paper used – better still, do away with delegate packs and provide documents on CD or memory sticks. Ensure that you promote to the guests ways to reach the location on foot, along with transport links and websites which enable the guest to have more options. When considering an event management team, contemplate whether it is feasible for them to car share or, if arriving by public transport, see if they can share transport to the location. When arranging subsistence for personnel and suppliers, liaise with the location to ensure that all meals are healthy and nutritious, utilising fresh, seasonal produce and, instead of providing bottled water, arrange for jugs of tap water. Wherever possible use natural daylight and natural ventilation and when considering striking after the event, pre-arrange recycle bins and collection points. There are so many aspects of an event that you can consider and I would urge you to read in full the BS 8901 document – although it may not be possible to do everything suggested in the guide, every little helps!

When you have examined how to reduce the event's carbon footprint, arrange to have a meeting with the location to discuss how, together, you can create a more sustainable event. Likewise, encourage suppliers and event personnel to also become actively involved and share your objectives with them. Regardless of the event whether this be a party, conference, awards ceremony, team build, activity day, press & product launch or family fun day, full consideration should be given. Finally, put your sustainable measures in place.

As you become used to organising events, you may find that you wear your 'environment' hat right from the onset and consider all aspects at an earlier stage. I personally think that as much as we all now consider H&S as part and parcel of staging an event, in time, we shall all consider the importance of creating a 'sustainable' event in a similar way.

So, that's your logistics, sustainability and event management sorted. You have just a few more organisational duties to perform prior to moving on to the event finalisation and these include:

Car Parking

Establishing deliveries and car park requirements for the suppliers and on site personnel is important if you want this element to run smoothly. Unloading can be hazardous and, as such, it is best to schedule and stagger delivery times wherever possible. Identify *who* and *what time* they are arriving along with the vehicle details, including registration numbers, and forward this information to the location to keep it abreast of the situation. Where relevant, try to negotiate with the location regarding car parking fees - they will sometimes reduce rates.

Celebrations

During the course of the event, you may find that the brief provider will want to say a few words of thanks. You may need to organise some flowers for fellow colleagues (they may wish to do this for you, you never know) or you may need to organise a Birthday cake to be available to present to a guest. You still need to factor this aspect into the format, how embarrassing would it be if the host stood up to thank someone and the flowers were nowhere to be seen– this type of seemingly impromptu display of thanks actually needs quite precise planning!

Top Tip Tick:

If you are arranging for a Birthday cake or flowers, make sure that when they are delivered they are placed in cool storage. Icing sweats and flowers wilt in heat so try to keep them in tip top condition.

Petty Cash

If you haven't done so already, you need to calculate if you are likely to require any petty cash. It is always advisable to take some with you as there can be many an occurrence that arises where someone has to dash out to the shops to get something prior to the event, so take more than you need. Also I tend to factor in 'tipping'.

At the end of the event, if the location's staff have been helpful, friendly and generally pleasant and proactive to work with, I like to provide a tip to be split between all the personnel that worked on the event.

Transportation

When you have considered the aspects you will be personally taking to the location – also consider hiring a van if necessary. Arrange a van large enough to cope but small enough to park in the available parking areas. Never, ever, underestimate the amount of space that items such as theming, prizes and plastic boxes can take up in a vehicle.

Final Costing

Now that the logistics have all been considered, it is the time to undertake your final costing just to ensure that you are still very much on target.

Top Tip Tick:

When finalising the logistics and the accurate costing, remember to read each of the suppliers' terms and conditions carefully. In particular, if hiring the services of a band there is a good chance that they will have a Rider. A Rider is basically everything the band or the band's management/agent need with which to agree to perform. This can be a production requirement such as a stage or a public address system and band/crew subsistence which can be very specific indeed. So do take this into account, especially when scheduling and also budgeting.

As a rule of thumb, where drinks are concerned, providing a range of cold soft drink and tea/coffee is more than acceptable but depending upon the entertainer's or band's status, they may be more specific and ask for beer, wine and even Champagne to be provided just prior to and during their performance. If this is the case then you need to arrange this to be placed into their dressing/function room but if you wish to generally provide any alcoholic beverages, unless it is specified as a Rider requirement, try to arrange this for after their performance.

Regular suppliers such as close hand magicians are normally more than happy with a meal such as a Shepherds Pie or some filling sandwiches, water, orange juice and hot drinks – unless their subsistence requirements are specifically detailed in their terms and conditions.

Your final and accurate Event Costing for this fictional event, may very well now look like this.

Top Tip Tick:

There is no better feeling than highlighting a task from your To Do List – ticking it off the list. This process will provide a sense of great satisfaction that you are winning and getting there. And, when you see that there is more 'black' than 'coloured' text on the Itinerary, it will give you an added sense of satisfaction and achievement.

You are now at that stage where there are just a few more ticks to make on your To Do List and you must be close to finalising your Itinerary – believe me it will feel so good, so persevere!

Event Finalisation

That's the Event organisation complete right? Well, you are nearly there but before you can categorically state that you are 100% organised, take a look at the Ultimate Tick List to make certain that you have considered *absolutely* everything!

So, we are now approaching the event finalisation stage as you prepare to take everything necessary with you on site but first...

When you have checked that you are completely organised, scan through your Event Itinerary and finalise this document. Just double check that you have updated the Itinerary with the revised final numbers (as there will be many revisions) along with any changes to rooming lists and dietary requirements for the guests, crew, internal personnel, suppliers and on site management and disseminate this information to the location. (Send the Itinerary to the location minus contact details or anything of a confidential nature – it would be best to ask the location when it issues its own internal function sheets, its own in house itinerary, and try to ensure that you forward a copy to them prior to this date.)

Likewise, it is always wise to forward by email a copy of the complete Itinerary to anyone who plays an active role on site (this includes suppliers where applicable). Although I always print out hard copies for all event managers and schedule a production meeting prior to the guests' arrival, the sooner they receive a copy the sooner they can identify what is expected of them and familiarise themselves with the event.

Top Tip Tick:

When finalising details, contact the location and request a Production Meeting to take place as soon as you have unloaded and settled into your base. At this meeting, you can double check the running order of the event with the location's key personnel.

Then, prior to binding the Itineraries, you need to add to the back some key forms of documentation such as:

- Rooming list (if applicable)
- Alphabetical guest list (indicating those guests with special dietary needs)
- Table plan
- Contact list of all suppliers including mobile numbers
- Blank lined paper for the copious amounts of notes you will take throughout

When these have been bound, you should place all key documents onto a memory stick or disc and take your hard copies of any key contracts etc. If relevant, take copies of any various insurance policies and details with you and pack up your laptop.

Should you have an event team working with you, if you haven't arranged this through the designated design and print supplier, create some ID badges – I tend to create reusable badges for each team member, including the crew, as this helps the location and will aid your boss, colleague or client to easily identify specific personnel.

Working through your Itinerary, start creating a tick list of everything you need to take with you and pack everything into durable plastic storage boxes, mark the top of the lids clearly with a list of the enclosures and number of boxes in total.

So, you have now concluded the organisation by fully contemplating the on site logistics. Your administrative housekeeping is well kept, you have managed your Benchmark Schedule, you are completely up to date with your Event Itinerary, highlighted all tasks off your To Do List and you are all ready and packed.

Now that you have mastered how to THINK like a proficient event organiser are you ready to ACT like one?

CHAPTER 5

Production – On Site

Production – On Site

Well done, you've made it…

In true proficient event organiser form, you are on site prior to anyone else - be prepared for, in this fictional case, a long day and night!

You will have calculated the time that you needed to arrive at the location, after contemplating the many duties to be undertaken on site and you have established how you and any event team would get to the location - the chances are, for an evening event, you will have planned to arrive early in the morning, allowing you and the team ample time to prepare.

The first thing to do when you arrive is to unload into your production office (if you have one) followed by consuming a strong cup of coffee. Well, it works for me. Whilst drinking your coffee, ascertain if you need any additional tables and chairs so that you can settle yourself in nicely and make the area that you and any event team shall be working within as comfortable and user friendly as possible.

As the key event organiser and manager you will have scheduled a meeting with the location's conference and banqueting team to go through in fine detail, your and their understanding of the running order for the event.

Banqueting Team Meeting

At this meeting, you may be introduced to your Banqueting Manager(s) who is dedicated to the event for the duration. (There may be two personnel depending upon their shift patterns.) This is the time that you will need to refer to your Event Itinerary which will by now have detailed absolutely everything relating to the event within the body of the document.

The purpose of this meeting is for all parties to agree to the agenda and to finalise any outstanding details. The discussions should also include, where relevant:

- To arrange for the location to keep you informed of the drink allocation when guests consume close to any budget set. I tend to ask a location to inform me when the guests have consumed within 10%

of the allocated amount so that I can seek clarification from the brief provider or person paying the bill whether he/she wishes to extend the allocation or keep to the original plan of, say, reverting to a cash bar when the limit is reached.

• It is also advisable to discuss with the location how situations will be dealt with should some rowdy behaviour occur. They will have a policy in place to deal with general unacceptable behaviour and verbal or physical abuse so it is best for you and any event team to be aware of how the location will deal with such situations should they arise.

• You may be able to arrange for late checkouts for any key personnel staying overnight. These personnel are normally the event managers and crew who tend to work much later than anyone else attending an event.

• If the circumstances govern, I ask the location at this meeting to confirm key H&S information such as: who is their dedicated first aider (during the set up and event itself) and the details of the location's GP. I'd also enquire of the location's evacuation procedures and the address of the closest hospital. I always ensure that this information is disseminated to the event managers so that in case of an incident they are aware of the procedures.

Top Tip Tick:

Should a medical incident/evacuation arise this would normally be handled by the location.

• Finally, as well as reconfirming timings and details of the event, one question that should be clarified with the location, if not discussed before, is how they are going to deal with 'dietary requirements'. If there is a formal table plan, this is normally not a problem as you will have previously informed the location which guest has a special dietary need and they can be identified by means of a floor plan and the guests' place card. This gets a bit trickier when a table plan is not provided. If this circumstance should arise, you will need to work hand in hand with the location and help to identify the guest(s) and where they are seated – it's not ideal but it normally works out fine.

Top Tip Tick:

When at a production meeting with the location, discuss forms of communication during the event period. Many changes and last minute requests will still undoubtedly arise during the event and you will need to be able to quickly contact your designated Banqueting Manager. Some locations will provide an in-house mobile event phone or a land-line in your production office along with notification of a direct extension number – personally, I like to provide my contact with one of the two way radios, this way the Banqueting Manager can be kept aware of what is going on at all times and be instantly contactable.

Once the event has been discussed in detail and actions agreed upon, after concluding the Production Meeting, one other form of documentation should be completed.

Risk Assessment documents will have been requested from any applicable suppliers contracted for the event and, as a legal requirement, the location will have undertaken its own intensive 'generic' risk assessments based on its premises and, should the necessity have arisen, will undoubtedly have flagged up any potential H&S issues during the planning of the event. Nonetheless, should circumstances dictate, whereby additional event managers are working on site, I undertake a 'dynamic' risk assessment of the areas that the guests and the event team will be utilising.   (See Chapter 7 for further details.)

Top Tip Tick:

Regardless of whether any additional event managers are working on the event, it is advisable to undertake a dynamic risk assessment anyway as, according to the H&S at Work Act, you are responsible for your own safety (as well as the safety of those around you).

That's the paperwork completed…the next meeting to have is with the event management team, should there be more than one of you managing the event. Assuming there is…

Event Management Meeting

Once back at your base, the next job is to sort out the radios. I like to have them labelled with each person's name to easily identify a radio(s) should it be misplaced – I tend to do this by writing on a sticky label and securing it to the handset. It is also normally best that all radios are tuned to channel one, but in busy areas, you may actually pick up taxi cab conversation so select the most appropriate channel whilst also taking into account any channel restrictions that may apply to your particular hand sets.

It's time to distribute the all important two way radios and covert ear pieces along with the Event Itinerary and highlighter pens from your Tool Box. You should go through the Itinerary together, remembering that this may be the very first time that the other event managers have seen the location so up on to your feet and walk the team through the event, starting at the front door. (Take this opportunity to test out the radios as not all event managers may be familiar with the mechanics.)

You will have assigned specific duties for each event manager within the Itinerary and when you all finally sit back down together, ask each event manager to identify their own duties and mark these with a highlighter pen, this way they will be able to see at a glance *when* and *what* they are responsible for undertaking. This is also the time when the event team should be briefed with any relevant H&S points raised from the completion of the Dynamic Risk Assessment. (Again, see Chapter 7 for further information.)

Setting up

You may not feel hungry during the set up period as you may be running on nervous energy but keeping yourself hydrated and fed is extremely important if you are 'running the show' – make a conscious effort to eat and drink plenty of water on a regular basis. Arrange to have a bowl of fruit placed in your production office, in particular *bananas* are great as these will keep you going, especially when you may possibly run out of time to sit down and eat an entire meal.

When everything appears to be ready, this is the time for double and quadruple checking, especially when it comes to table settings. If the location has been given the task of positioning the place cards on the table, either yourself or a member of the event management team will need to check each table to ensure that the cards have been placed exactly according to the table plan. At the same time, you will need to verify that each place setting has the right number of glasses, complete set of cutlery, a napkin, side plate and even a chair – make certain that the placement of all elements are replicated precisely for each setting, everything has to be just so. If it isn't, lean the chair forward (assuming there is one in its desired place) onto the table which will clearly indicate which specific table setting needs to be addressed.

During the set up period, keep on top of all suppliers and make sure that they are aware of the impending guests' arrival time. Try to aim to get everything completely ready at least thirty – forty five minutes prior to the anticipated arrival time of the guests as there are always, always some early arrivals.

Top Tip Tick:

I find that it is best to try to organise for the brief provider to arrive on site as late as possible – half an hour before the guests are scheduled to arrive is perfect rather than any earlier. Understandably, people can flap a little when there seems so much to achieve within such a short time frame. Part of your job is to keep your boss, colleague or client calm and reassure him/her as much as you possibly can that everything will be 'alright on the night' and will most certainly be ready in time for the guests' arrival.

Ready to Go!

Right, everything is set up, the whole team is changed and ready for action. Last minute checks undertaken - this paints a lovely picture doesn't it? Everything serene, everything ready…

The reality is, of course, more likely to be that you are all frantically running around tending to last minute changes to the table plan and trying to locate the missing place card, chasing up the DJ because he hasn't arrived yet to set up and working out with the location the best way to utilise an alternative entrance as the car park has flooded.

Top Tip Tick:

If you take an hour to get ready – this job may not be for you. Still keen? Then you will have to learn how to master the art of grabbing a quick refresher shower, change and reapply make up (should you be a lady) within a twenty minute slot.

Now, this is where you can experience the true benefit of having contemplated all the logistics and organising everything down to the finest of detail. Can you imagine having to continue to organise as well as deal proficiently with any high, low or curve ball - your brain would go into sensory overload. So, the reason why I suggest the event is organised to the finest of detail is so that you can deal competently with any unforeseen situations as they materialise and make changes to your management process where needs be. Just be prepared, that even with the most detailed of detailed planning, something out of the blue invariably happens, so my advice to you is to constantly monitor the event and, with the help of any event team, to address situations as they arise but do so with composure and in a calm manner.

What to Do When Things Don't Go to Plan!

Events very rarely go exactly to plan. As I have mentioned previously, it is how you deal with the situation. Even the most potential of disasters can be turned into nothing more than a blip, an unnoticed blip at that. There truly is not a list of tips that I can give you to magic away situations that you would prefer not to arise. My advice to you, nevertheless, is that there is always normally a solution to find but it is down to you as the team leader to do just that. Contemplate the best way forward and, where applicable, to *lead the team.*

Top Tip Tick:

If you strut around with a face like fizz or like a rabbit in the headlights of a car, then the guests will pick up on this. Always be aware that your face and your body language are speaking volumes, so keep these in check. The chances are that guests will not know if something has happened that shouldn't have, only you and any of the event team will know, so try to keep it that way.

Should an unforeseen situation arise and you are working with an event team, one of whom is getting flustered, take this person aside, remind them of the importance of keeping the right demeanour or get them to take 'five'. Stay calm within yourself and this should help you to make a good judgement call.

Obviously there are situations where there is simply nothing you can do and you know what, your boss, colleague, client or the guests will also appreciate that there is nothing you can do – these are situations way beyond your control so try not to be too hard on yourself should they occur. A fire alarm where the guests have to be evacuated – beyond your control. A power cut where all the conference equipment crashes – beyond your control. A guest faints in the middle of a presentation – beyond your control.

However, it's just as much about *how* you deal with the situation than the situation itself. Let's take the fire alarm scenario. Where you can be proactive, liaise with the location, keep guests informed and guide them as directed. A power cut – if safety allows and it looks like the cut is not a momentary issue, lead the guests to an alternative area where perhaps they could be served some drinks outside in the garden or under candlelight whilst waiting for the power to return… liaise with the location and be proactive, keep the guests informed. A guest faints – call the dedicated first aider promptly and, if possible, find the guest a more comfortable and private location in which to come round whilst the event recommences. Liaise with the location and keep the guests updated.

Top Tip Tick:

Should a medical incident occur during the course of an event, depending upon the circumstance, the contracting party or the location will need to complete an Accident Log. This is normally carried out by the person who actually administers first aid. The incident will need to be recorded and kept on file.

There are other aspects that may not be so obvious to the guests, such as a DJ not turning up when scheduled. You will have, regardless, factored into the Itinerary to check on the DJ during the course of the day that everything was going to plan. You would know his/her mobile number and you had arranged for him/her to arrive in plenty of time to set up so this would give you enough time to find a replacement or liaise with the location to serve the menu at a more leisurely pace in order to allow for the DJ to arrive if he/she has been unavoidably delayed. So really, it is all about just keeping the communication channels open.

So you see, when you have planned for the worst case scenario, the chances are you will be able to make the best out of the very worst situation. I remember organising a Fun Day for 300 people and the heavens opened from the moment the guests arrived until the moment they left. This meant that the guests had to be fed, watered and entertained under the cover of a marquee. In-depth planning had meant that the worst case scenario had been catered for so we knew that all guests could fit under one cover – it took great team work to entertain the guests in such a confined area but it was a situation beyond our control. We all did our best to make the most of the predicament and the guests still had a great day, a wet day, but nonetheless an enjoyable time was had by all.

Working in advance

When working from your Itinerary, you will be able to clearly see what should be happening in the background at any given time. Good event management is all about working in advance.

The beauty of the Event Itinerary is that everyone who is helping to produce and manage the event will know what their duties are from the moment they set foot on site to the moment they depart. So you will never have anyone just standing around waiting to be told what they should be doing. You may need to nudge the event team during the course of the function to make sure that they are keeping abreast of their duties and you may also like to check if they have undertaken certain tasks as featured within the Itinerary but you, as the team leader, should certainly not be instructing them what to do at this stage.

The duties contemplated will ensure that any event managers will be working well in advance of the various aspects of the event just to make sure that everything is perfect and ready for the guests, every step of the way. (And, when everything is looking super don't be too upset if you have themed the room to perfection and then as soon as the guests enter and sit down, arrangements get pulled apart and balloons are popped. That's just guests' high spirits. The most important thing was that it looked good when guests first entered the area.)

Let us refer to the fictional event for a moment…if the guests are supposed to be moving into dinner at 20.15, you or a member of the event team would need to check at 20.00 that the location staff are all up to speed and that the level of lighting in the room is as it should be, the candles are lit and that the background music is playing. All event managers should also be in their positions i.e. lining the route, at their designated time, and to be on hand to direct guests to their allocated tables. Always, always work in advance so that help and guidance can readily be offered.

Top Tip Tick:

Just because a location has had a meeting with you to discuss all timings, never assume that they will run to schedule. Working in advance and checking with your Banqueting Manager to see if they are working to time is an important role to undertake. You don't have to constantly be 'in their face' but you do need to be working hand in hand with them and keep on top of the situation. If there is a delay in the kitchen, then try to keep your head and just delay moving the guests through to the next location until the kitchen's ready – it's all about team work.

Event Management

Remember, you are there to work. I know that this is a very obvious thing to say but I have been told by many a client of occasions where a member of their staff had organised an event so fantastically well but when it came to the event itself, sheer relief overcame them, coupled with a few celebratory glasses of bubbly and, well, the organiser just fell to pieces, which resulted in the bosses themselves having to ensure that everything ran smoothly for the rest of the event.

Of course if you are contracted as an event organiser then this situation wouldn't arise but so many people let themselves down by organising the event proficiently and then totally relaxing on site when this is exactly where they need to be on their toes. In many ways, this is where the hard work truly begins.

Make no doubt about it, working on site is stressful. Keeping a good sense of humour throughout is probably the best piece of advice that I can give to you. When things get tough or you feel stressed, take five minutes out. Breathe, count to ten and reach for the bottle – bottle or jug of water that is!

Top Tip Tick:

I always ensure that eating is taken in shifts so that there is at least one event manager overseeing the guests. Generally, the event team should either be preparing the next phase of the event or maintaining a presence where the guests are situated so to be on hand at all times.

End of Event

As the event draws to a close, you may indeed be looking at your watch, (especially if there is a deadline to be clear of the room) but don't be surprised if the event does over-run slightly. Although locations are pretty hot on events finishing at the time specified on the contract, you can't afford to let up until the very last guest has departed the event. Even if your feet are desperately aching and you wouldn't mind a glass of that wine that the guests have been drinking and, well, you really *love* the song that the DJ is presently playing and even with sore feet you are dying to get on that dance floor and let your hair down - after all you do deserve it! Of course you deserve it but managing the guests from the moment they arrive to the moment they leave is all part and parcel of what we do. You must stay focused.

Hopefully, the guests will have had a lovely time and you want to ensure that their last memory of the event remains positive to the end. At an event similar to our fictional example, some guests may get lost and experience difficulty in finding their way out (which happens more times than you may imagine). They may not be able to find the ticket for their coat and are slightly too worse for wear to deal with it – you must be there to help wherever needs be.

One of the last and sometimes most difficult of tasks to undertake is to tactfully move those guests who may seem to be glued to their chairs, either on their way or into a secondary area where they can continue to relax and enjoy the other guests' company – this takes diplomacy, much smiling and much patience but if you can stir them to make a move so the location staff can start clearing the room safely, all the better. This will also allow you to assign any event management personnel to start striking this room should there be enough staff on hand to also guide and help guests as they prepare to depart.

When guests do finally depart, make sure that the designated event management team 'line the route' as much as possible and make it clear to guests that they can willingly take away with them any disposable theming such as the balloons and the table displays, should they be free of any hired elements. Direct the guests to the exit, be on hand to assist and finally thank them for coming and wish them a safe journey home. Lasting, positive impressions.

So now all the guests have gone, the time has come to have that glass of wine and put your feet up, right? No chance! Time to 'strike', take down directional signs, collect the radios and any reusable items such as personnel badging, dismantle theming and empty the production office etc. When all this has been done, to celebrate the ultimate final ticking off the list, then you and any event team can all have a well earned glass of wine or two.

Top Tip Tick:

Some locations ask for a Security Deposit. This deposit is to be utilised should any damage occur to the location as a direct result of suppliers or guests attending the event. I find that it is always best to arrange, with the hotel management, for a 'dilapidation tour' prior to and after the event so that any damage can be either eliminated or accessed and agreed upon there and then.

And finally, when you are scheduling, if the event does run late into a night/early morning, do try to bear in mind how tired you and any event team will feel and what time you will actually finish. As previously mentioned, it is always advisable to book accommodation within the location or a hotel close by so that you or any team member do not have to drive and can just climb into bed before sinking into a deep, much earned, sleep.

Life as a proficient event organiser…is great, but very, very tiring!

Prior to Departure

Always make an effort before you leave the location, no matter whether this be in the middle of the night, in the early hours of the morning or the following day, to meet with your banqueting team to provide some preliminary feedback and, of course, thank them should they have provided a great service.

All being well, the location will have provided an excellent service but if this is not the case you may need to let them know that you will be in contact to arrange for a follow up meeting to take place where you can air any disappointment or cause for complaint.

However, should you have been happy with the service that you received, this is the time you should give a tip to your contact and ask if they can divide the monies between all the personnel that worked on the event. This way, everyone gets a little thank you.

Top Tip Tick:

When you are planning make sure that you ask the location when the function room(s) have to be clear. The majority of locations normally wish for the facilities to be cleared immediately so that the space is free for other clients that may be coming in straight after the event you have managed. Whatever is confirmed, make sure that you have communicated this requirement to all suppliers.

Also, when it comes to disposing of rubbish, some locations specify that this is the responsibility of the person/company who generated it in the first place. Much unwanted material such as pages from delegate packs or theming containers can be taken care of by sorting them into recycling bins but for those items that are not recyclable, it is important to consider how best to deal with and schedule their disposal.

One final note of warning… Data Protection. Be mindful of the rubbish that you are removing. If it is of a sensitive nature ensure that it is disposed of in a method fitting to Data Protection guidelines.

Do be warned that if you inadvertently leave something in a function room or production office that you wanted to keep, chances are that it will ultimately be disposed off by the location staff straight after the function. It is no good phoning up the location two days later and asking if they still have the flip chart pad that your boss, colleague or client happened to be using… they have probably had a further three, or so, events in after you!

CHAPTER 6

Post Production

Post Production

Well, you should now be feeling elated. Exhausted but elated! All the hard work over…

Final Costing

Time now to sort out your documents and undertake a final costing. Hopefully, you will have been updating your costing spreadsheet as and when amendments arose, so this shouldn't be too much of a trauma to undertake. You will need to wait for the location's invoice and all of the suppliers' invoices prior to signing off the final costing and ensure that you check all invoices carefully prior to authorising them for payment. If you have maintained good administrative housekeeping, then there truly should be no surprises at this stage.

Top Tip Tick:

During your liaison with a location, always ask how they will execute their final bill. What I mean by this is that you need to get an agreement from them with regards to the time scale involved, what the layout will look like and reiterate that you wish for the billing to be simple to read and easy to clarify with all dockets relating to the event present along with the breakdown of costings.

Locations' final invoices are the bane of my life… you get used to their contract and function sheet layout and then normally their final bill bears absolutely no resemblance to any documents that you have seen previously so it's like starting from scratch and can be an overwhelming task to check through.

During my twenty one years of event organising, unfortunately I have only had a handful of final bills that have been 100% accurate and so my advice to you is to check everything carefully. I used to spend a great deal of time to-ing and fro-ing between the location's accounts department and the banqueting manager and now if I have any queries after my initial digestion of the final bill, I make an appointment to go through the bill face to face. This way, the bill gets clarified much, much quicker which is better for them and better for you.

If at all possible, endeavour to get invoices settled as quickly as possible. First of all you will gain yourself, your boss, colleague or client a positive reputation in the industry for being a good/prompt payer.

Secondly, suppliers are more likely to provide flexibility when needed in the future if you have looked after them in the past and thirdly, a *paid* supplier is a *happy* supplier and a happy supplier will always be happy to work with you in the future. Remember, event organisation is not just a 'one off' activity, it is very important to strike up many quality relationships with a variety of suppliers so that you can freely draw upon their services in the future.

Thank you

Finally, if you felt that the location, any event management team and the supplier(s) did a good job, then take some time out to write to them and thank them for their support and service provided. Everyone likes to feel valued and a thank you letter is always very much appreciated.

File Management

Now all there is to do is to tidy everything away. As at the start of the organisational process, we all have our way of doing things. My way of closing a job is to place all the key documents into a large envelope (detailing the job on the front) and either shredding any other paperwork, including all bar one of the itineraries, or reusing non confidential paper for drafts. Any items in the recycle box, I sort accordingly. Then I place all the email and word documents on to a CD ROM and I keep the Itinerary in a safe place. This way, if asked to arrange another event for the same client, then I can easily refer to the exact content and format of the previous occasion.

I then create two documents which are a Debrief document and a Suppliers document. The first is basically a report on how the event ran, so should my client require a debrief at a later stage, everything can remain, with a little amount of memory jogging, fresh in my mind. The Suppliers document is similar to the Debrief document but details how the suppliers performed, which is helpful for future events to determine whether I would utilise or guide a client to utilise a supplier again.

So that truly is the final tick off your list – happy now? You certainly should be. If you have followed the step by step process, you should definitely be patting yourself firmly on the back and so will your boss, colleague or client – what an accomplished and proficient event organiser you indeed are!

Top Tip Tick:

You may like to propose to the person hosting the event that they utilise photographs (should they have had a photographer) to create a commemorative gift of the event by means of a publication created in the style of a popular magazine. Alternatively, if budget is not available, then photographs could be placed onto a website for guests to visit or you could suggest sending guests a commemorative photo of the occasion.

CHAPTER 7

Health and Safety

Health and Safety

Health & Safety (H&S) plays an important role in the organisation of events. It is crucial that you understand the legal requirements and *who* has *what* responsibility.

Event Organisers

As a Consultant, I have both Public Liability and Professional Indemnity Insurance cover. Your insurance requirements will vary depending upon the nature of your employment. To check on your own personal legal requirements, I would suggest you seek professional advice. (Guidance can be found within the Helpful Contact Details section featured at the back of this book.)

Suppliers

As previously mentioned, all suppliers should have adequate Public Liability insurance. The amount of cover depends upon the service the supplier is providing. (Between £2m and £5m.)

Consequently, you would probably anticipate that a close hand magician is deemed as a low risk supplier whereas a fire-eater is likely to be deemed as a high risk supplier. This is, in fact, not a correct assumption. Cover is assessed on many aspects of a performance but as a rule, its primary concern is for the wellbeing of the 'audience'. For example, a close hand magician is likely to have many props in close proximity to the guests and as such the risk may be assessed higher for him/her than it would be for a fire-eater who is likely to have limited props and performing at a safe distance. So the level of insurance cover may reflect accordingly.

When requesting proof of insurance, the supplier may forward a copy of their Employers Liability certificate but what needs to be inspected, in this particular instance, is their 'schedule' which details their Public Liability Cover. An individual entertainer or sole trader is more than likely just going to have the Public Liability cover rather than Employers Liability – this is perfectly acceptable as it is the Public Liability cover for which assurance is required.

Also in accordance with H&S, it is always advisable to query the provision of their Risk Assessment document. If the supplier is a 'one man band' and self employed it may be deemed unreasonable to expect them to have their own Risk Assessment (unless their trade is hazardous by nature ie involving electrics etc). However, if an employer has more than five employees, the company is legally bound to have a H&S policy which would include all applicable Risk Assessments.

Indeed, some locations request to see all suppliers' Risk Assessments prior to agreeing to their participation, so be prepared. At the end of the day, I always, always, err on the side of caution.

Location

As a rule of thumb, if a standard location is contracted, the location is responsible to undertake and/or produce: a) fire risk assessment – completed under regularity reform order, b) H&S risk assessment for the associated event ie 'generic' RA and c) general H&S policy of their location. It is, nevertheless, your responsibility, should you be the contracting party (the person authorised and signatory on a contract) to ask to see copies of all these documents, check them and retain on file.

Should you, however, be working similarly to myself whereby the client signs all contracts with the location (and suppliers) it is then your responsibility to *advise* your clients to ask to see such documentation, check and to retain on file. For the avoidance of doubt, the individual or company that enters into a formal agreement with a location (or supplier) is termed as the 'contracting' party. (Where Suppliers Risk Assessments are concerned, should you be the 'contracting' party then you would ask to see these documents and retain them on file. If you are not the 'contracting' party then you would advise the contracting party, similar to the location information, to obtain this information direct from the suppliers.)

(The only exception to the aforementioned is if the contracting party 'dry' hire a vessel such as a yacht without a skipper or location such as a farmer's field where the location's main use differs from the use requested. Basically, this is where the contracting party would be responsible to carry out various dynamic risk assessments although the suppliers will have completed their own risk assessments and, depending upon the circumstance, a fire assessment - this will form part of the contract for hire.)

Top Tip Tick:

If you are the 'organiser' but not the 'contracting' party, you may find yourself in the situation where you are liaising directly with the location and all suppliers relating to the event and it is not practical for the contracting party to gather all the required information. In this circumstance and although it remains the contracting party's responsibility, 'on behalf' of the contracting party, I tend to gather all documents (Insurance and Risk Assessments) and send to the contracting party to check and to retain on file. Sometimes, practicalities have to be considered.

On Site

As mentioned in Chapter 5, a dynamic risk assessment needs to be completed should additional event management personnel be working on site. The information gleaned would be disseminated to the event team and potentially to the guests at the start of the event to ensure their safety.

It is the responsibility of the contracting party to undertake the dynamic risk assessment but practicalities normally dictate that you as the event organiser would undertake this role (regardless of whether you are or are not the contracting party).

Although I have personally taken guidance from an H&S professional to enable myself to competently undertake risk assessments of this nature, before you panic, undertaking a risk assessment at this level is just a matter of basic common sense.

By utilising a Severity x Probability Table in conjunction with a Dynamic Risk Assessment Form, I tend to walk the route and just look around taking note of, say, the condition of the carpet. Are there any rips that should be brought to the attention of the location which could cause a guest to trip? Are there any directional signs on stands, the legs of which are causing a hazard?

Top Tip Ticks:

Where situations allow, at the beginning of the event, I suggest to my clients that they inform their guests of the location's: evacuation procedures, fire exit locations, general relevant policies, what to do if anyone should need medical attention and also to draw to the guests' attention any specific hazards. My 'pointer' form may include statements such as 'please be mindful that the steps leading to the conservatory may be slippy due to the rain' etc. You may also like to suggest that they, in addition, point out general 'housekeeping' at the same time, i.e. the location of toilets. This type of information is compiled from information provided by the location during the banqueting team meeting along with details highlighted when undertaking the 'dynamic' risk assessment.

Presently there is no legal requirement for the hosts of an event to make this general H&S announcement, although legislation changes on a regular basis. Legislation does, however, state that the host of the function has a 'duty of care' to anyone in their charge. Regardless, I think that it is a courteous action to undertake even if it is not presently a 'legal' requirement.

NB: It is the responsibility of the contracting party to establish the information that should be announced to their guests. As a Consultant, i.e. not the contracting party, I provide 'pointers' but at the end of the day, the contracting party should decide on the information disseminated.

My findings are then documented and where relevant the details shared with the event managers, just to ensure that I have prepared for the guests arrival to the best of my abilities and that my, and the event managers safety, had been fully contemplated. I would advise that you seek guidance from an expert who will direct you on how to undertake basic risk assessments, provide and complete the forms – it doesn't cost a great deal of money but the knowledge that you will gain could be invaluable.

So to reiterate…

A *generic* risk assessment undertaken by a location would be for instance 'a conference for 220 people', 'a disco for 100 people' a 'generic' event if you like. A *dynamic* risk assessment is what the contracting party or you as the event organiser would perform at the time of the event i.e. specific to the event, highlighting such issues as a torn carpet which would cause a trip hazard to the event team or guests attending the event.

H&S Adviser

Sounds like a bit of a minefield, this H&S business, doesn't it? Well the truth of the matter is that it is! There may be situations where you are organising a straight forward event and dealing just with a hotel that readily has all the documents mentioned, with no additional suppliers, but my advice to you is, wherever you can, build in the services of a H&S adviser.

The H&S adviser should ideally be NEBOSH general certificate accredited and have in place both Public Liability and Professional Indemnity Insurance★.

He or she would take the responsibility off your or the 'contracting' party's shoulders and place firmly on to theirs. You can contract a H&S adviser to just liaise with the location and suppliers during the pre production phase to ensure that all parties are complying with H&S regulations (obtaining the necessary insurance details, plans and risk assessments) and if you felt that you would like to have this person on site to act as the dedicated H&S manager, you could extend their contractual period. Their duties could then include: meeting with the location re evacuation procedures, the undertaking of the 'dynamic' risk assessment and briefing you and the event managers, provide guidance on content or undertake the H&S announcement at the beginning of the event and to be on hand should anything arise such as a medical incident or evacuation. So, really, for a relatively small investment, this will provide you and your boss, colleague or client with absolute peace of mind.

★ Professional Indemnity Insurance covers a consultant in case he/she offers incorrect advice and therefore provides added security for the entity securing such services.

A Word to the Wise

In order to highlight the level of importance that you should be placing on H&S, I would like to share a situation that I have had the misfortune to experience once in my career – hopefully, this will demonstrate why you should treat all aspects relating to H&S with the highest of importance.

Within my twenty one years of event organising, I am thankful to say that I have only experienced one situation that could have ended in disaster. I hasten to add that this situation did not end in this manner, but, oh, it could so easily have done. So, I want to share with you my one and only significant 'heart leaping into the mouth' moment.

A new client asked my company to theme their prestigious car show room window for the Christmas period and had such great ideas of what they wished to achieve. To cut a very long story short, it was finally ascertained that they didn't have anywhere near the budget to accomplish what they wanted to do but to help secure a future relationship, it was decided that we would do whatever we could for them at a much reduced price.

It took many weeks to get to this stage and with Christmas ever looming and the launch of a car approaching quicker than you could say 'Father Christmas', it was agreed that a simple drape and lighting design would suffice.

A supplier was approached to provide and erect the draping and lighting at very short notice and when it was set up, having seen the powerful lights being utilised to cast the best light onto one of the glorious cars, I made a comment along the lines of 'This drape has been fire-treated hasn't it?' I was informed that it had been and if there were any unforeseen situations, it was likely to *smoulder* rather than burst into flames. 'Little consolation', I thought and although the clients didn't have the budget, I decided that *smoulder* was not good enough, I wanted it to be totally fire proofed. I decided to organise fire proofing and for my company to cover the costs - a small price to pay for peace of mind. This was now late into the evening but I arranged with the supplier for the drape to be treated first thing the following morning. After liaising with the client, all the display lights were turned off and all was set for the day. Unbeknown to us, in-between times, security arrived in the early hours and turned the lights on – apparently, as the front door opened, this caused a breeze which lifted the drape directly onto a display light (which, of course, is what happened to Windsor Castle!).

There the drape stayed and *smouldered*, as the supplier had indeed stated – panic, however, set in and the security person let rip with a fire extinguisher which promptly blasted the smouldering curtain onto the open topped display car, damaging the vehicle in the process. The only consolation being that the fire extinguisher chucked out foam at a remarkable rate and did the job with vigour.

When I received the call, I nearly collapsed. I recall hearing the horrifying words, 'there has been a fire' and I don't remember a lot else! It turned out that there hadn't been a true fire but the effect was just as devastating, as was the aftermath. After collecting my scattered senses, I gathered my team and drove like the wind to central London where I witnessed nothing short of a disaster scene. The fire extinguisher had left its mark in more ways than one, which resulted in all the cars having to be emptied out of the show room and heavy duty domestic cleaners brought in to clean up the mess.

The irony of it all was, as I was surveying the damage, there was a sheepish knock at the door and a young lad crooked his head around the entrance, with equipment in hand… 'I've come to… fireproof a…curtain…' he hesitantly announced.

This was where damage limitation and crisis management came into play. The car showroom personnel were clearing out the cars, the main car was being switched with an alternative model, the cleaners were, well, *cleaning* and my team had to not only dispense with the remaining theming but to totally re theme as a press launch was due to take place less than eight hours from our impromptu arrival time. Drape, don't mention that word… I assigned each person to a specific task, we called upon our suppliers left right and centre and once the showroom was clean, we got to work and started theming all over again, this time by utilising everything that was clearly fire proofed.

The showroom truly looked splendid after the team had finished – a true testament to great team work. The press arrived, blissfully unaware of the trauma that had led to that very moment. The showroom was happy, well, as happy as it could be under the circumstances and my hairdresser was happy as there was yet another grey hair for him to colour.

The moral of this story is, if the client hasn't got the budget to do what they want to do and safely, be strong enough to walk away. I've learned that lesson. But without exception, no matter whether suppliers are providing themselves as entertainers, as a service or equipment, ensure that they abide strictly with H&S pertaining to the provision of their service and that you, too, are quite clear of your legal requirements as the event organiser. H&S regulations have come a long way since this situation, which happened over a decade ago and so suppliers and, indeed, event organisations have to now abide by far stricter guidelines.

One other point that I should mention. Both my company and the supplier in question had healthy insurance cover in place and the situation was sorted professionally and amicably with the least amount of fuss. Imagine, if I had contracted suppliers that didn't have adequate insurance cover – well, it doesn't bear thinking about, does it?

So, I think by now you are getting a clearer picture of how imperative it is to fully consider H&S and how important, if budget and situations allow, it is to contract the services of a H&S adviser. As mentioned before, he or she can be asked to liaise with the location and any relevant suppliers during the pre production phase and be the main point of contact for all H&S aspects pertaining to the event whilst on site, along with briefing the event team. This is always my preferred option as it is one less thing to worry about.

CHAPTER 8

Components and Considerations

Components and Considerations

The previous pages of this book have provided the necessary steps to take to ensure a well prepared and managed event.

Basically, you should apply the principles of the step by step process for any style event. Conversely, as I am sure that you can appreciate, each type of function has unique considerations. Here are a few of the key aspects that you may also like to contemplate when embarking on the organisation process for a variety of functions - you will see that some have more key consideration points than others.

Conferences

When considering a conference and the Pre Production 'innovation' stage, you may like to ponder upon the following:-

Questions & Vision

There are many questions you need to ask and clarify when considering a conference: the date, timings and guideline format of the event is required, as are the anticipated number of delegates likely to attend – this is probably the most crucial as without this information you simply cannot take your location search any further nor develop the conference in any shape or form.

You also need to identify the vision of the brief provider regarding aspects such as the desired anticipated set design along with the speaker support material which your boss, colleague or client anticipates utilising i.e. PowerPoint and video. You need to establish if there is going to be the potential need for a script writer or a master of ceremonies (MC). Whether there is going to be a guest speaker, a celebrity host or a motivational speaker and whether audience participation is required. You need to clarify if additional meeting rooms (breakout rooms) are also to be factored and whether the brief provider visualises, in the main conference room, the delegates sitting in Theatre style (chairs in rows) Classroom (chairs in rows with long tables placed in front) Herringbone (as previous but tables placed at angles) Cabaret (sitting around round tables – normally six delegates to a table seated in a crescent shape) U Shape (classroom style with tables joined to create an 'u' shape) Hollow Oblong (similar to U shape but with four sides) or Boardroom (sitting around one large table) and whether 'back' or 'front' projection is required.

Back & Front Projection

Back projection relates to where the video projector would be situated, if the room size allows for it. It is the preferred option as it is easier for the production company to rig the projector at a good working height, rather than suspend it from the ceiling – as could be the case if front projection were utilised.

The control position (i.e. computers, video players etc) could still be situated out front of the set. For general tidiness, video control would normally be located behind the set, but not always. Front projection would be used if the room were quite small and back projection was not an option due to audience size. In this situation the control position would be out front. It should be noted that, in either scenario, any sound and lighting control location would be in front of the set, either at the back of the room or to one side.

If back projection is required this takes up more space of the overall room. As a rule of thumb, one and a half times the screen width would be the space that you would need to allow. So, if there was a screen which was 12ft (3.6m), this would require an 18ft (5.4m) projection distance.

Top Tip Tick:

More often than not, delegates sit Theatre style and for the purpose of identifying whether a location is large enough, I always ask to allow for back projection so, if, at the end of the day, the requirement is actually for front projection (which takes up less space) I can guarantee that there will be ample room.

When considering break out rooms, ensure that the room is large enough for its purpose and seating style. Contemplate whether it is anticipated that speaker support equipment i.e. any staging, lighting, sound, video projection and PowerPoint facilities would be needed.

Brief Document

When these questions have been contemplated, you can raise your initial Event Brief Document. The Event Brief can then be tweaked to bear relevance to the location, to create a Location Brief, and, secondly, amended for the production company producing the show (Production Brief).

Nevertheless, although the Location Brief is pretty straight forward, a Production Brief will probably be quite sketchy at the outset and, although it would be beneficial for all concerned to have the answers to many questions mentioned previously, so that the production company can provide an accurate quote, at the embryonic stage of a conference it is very rare that any kind of conference format or requirements can be confirmed.

So, as long as the initial Production Brief clarifies some key information such as: the date of the event, destination, guideline format, clarification of set up period available, indication of the type of set and anticipated speaker support material to be presented, along with an approximate budget, then the production company should be able to provide an initial guideline quote.

Once an updated Production Brief can be clarified i.e. when the conference format has been fully considered and requirements fully contemplated, that's when the Production Company will be able to provide a firm quote, so do bear this in mind when considering your overall event costing at this stage.

Top Tip Tick:

When studying the production company's firm quote, double check that they have included 'back up' equipment for aspects such as the show computer and projector(s). This will ensure that should a computer lock-up or a projector fail, the technician can seamlessly switch between equipment with little or no impact on the show.

Location Suitability

A location suitable for a conference may be very different from a location suitable for a dinner or a launch. There are some key factors that you need to ask a location at the outset and these include: the ceiling height, whether it has a pillar free environment, good load-in accessibility, black out facilities and adequate power supply.

Top Tip Tick:

When considering power supply, 'three phase' power is normally only required for events that utilise any form of theatrical lighting. For a small basic conference, power outlets around the room should be sufficient for sound and video equipment. If the event is quite large then 'single' or three phase power becomes a definite requirement. When considering power, you should also enquire as to where the power is fed from. For example, there may be a kitchen near to the conference room and when the ovens or dishwashers are turned on, power surges can occur. (It has happened!) A qualified venue technician should be able to answer these questions for you and allay any fears or flag up any potential situations.

Power supplies are one thing an event organiser or production company have little control over – you are relying on the location for this and if the power trips, so, unfortunately, can the show.

You also need to establish the location's maximum capacity based on the desired production and seating requirements i.e. Theatre style with back projection. As mentioned, ceiling height also needs to be checked. As a rule of thumb, a minimum ceiling height for a conference should ideally be in the region of 15ft or 4.57 metres (depending upon the style of presentation). It is also a good idea to check on the location's ISDN and Broadband capability within the main function room.

Top Tip Tick:

Once you have identified a potential location, ask the selected production company (see overleaf) to accompany you on a site visit so they can rubber stamp its suitability for the anticipated requirements prior to the location being formally confirmed.

Set up

When investigating, it is always a good idea to ascertain if the main conference room is available for 'set up' either two days or the day before the event.

Most conference schedules allow for set up of the equipment and the rehearsals to take place the day before the main event. If the budget is available, and depending upon the complexity of the conference itself, loading in the previous day/evening (to this) would always be preferred as this allows plenty of time for rehearsals, paramount for the presenters and production team alike.

A word of warning, however. Locations generally charge heavily for 'load in' room hire due to the fact that they need to compensate for loss of revenue that could have been generated from another alternative event which could have taken place during the set up period – you should establish exactly what these charges are at the outset and ensure that you factor this into your event costing.

Restrictions

So, having determined the key elements of the brief, also ask whether the location allows for confetti cannons, pyrotechnics and smoke – the production company would need to know this information should the brief provider wish to potentially incorporate any of these aspects within the event. (Locations will sometimes isolate detectors to enable smoke to be used to aid the overall lighting effect. It is, therefore, advisable to ask this question as there is not much use in planning the use of smoke if the alarms are likely to go off.)

Tweaking your Location Brief template to include these additional aspects will help to shortlist locations for your further consideration.

Benchmark Schedule & Itinerary

During the Pre Production 'organisation' phase, you will still be working from your Benchmark Schedule which should include various deadlines and duties relating to the conference production as well as the overall event organisation and also, of course, developing your Itinerary.

Supplier Selection

The best way of ensuring that you have considered everything involved with organising a conference is to secure a good production company or, as they can also be known, audio visual company.

There are many production companies in the UK and following the same process as you applied when securing a supplier would be my suggestion. Production companies very much vary on costs, charging anywhere between 10% – 25% of the production costs for their services. Remember, you generally get what you pay for.

Thus, most production companies will have their own show reel which is a video/DVD compilation of the events they have produced. Request a show reel and if you and the brief provider like what you see, take up the necessary references prior to securing their services.

Event Content and Time Line

Most production companies will be happy to offer advice and request the information that they need in order to take your requirement further and establish the event content. During the course of the organisational process they can assist you, your boss, colleague or client with the set design along with: lighting & sound, music, video production, presentation creation and general finalisation of the running order of the show. (They also hold, or can obtain, the necessary PRS licence to play music straight from CD live to the audience, for walk ups and music to visuals during a conference/awards ceremony.)

Top Tip Tick:

The selected production company will also inform you of the timeline in which all presentation material will need to be completed and forwarded to them. Most like to receive the complete show (including all scripts, PowerPoint presentations and video tapes) a few days before the event. This is so that they can familiarise themselves with the show, examine material to ensure all runs smoothly, double check that they have received everything that they should have and place the material into show order.

(Nonetheless, should anyone wish for autocue to be arranged, the production company will probably require the scripts and 'word' format version to be forwarded to them at an earlier stage.) When timings are known, make certain that you advise the brief provider of any critical timings well in advance.

Some production companies have the facilities to provide a full preview of the show. This is like a 'rehearsal' where each presenter can go through his/her presentation, viewing all slides and video prior to actually going on site. I would strongly recommend that if this facility is offered then this provision be willingly accepted so that personnel have the opportunity to go through their presentations and make any changes within the confines and flexibility of the production company's offices.

It is, however, a known fact that changes do take place at the last minute and most production companies will be able to make some changes on site but it is in everyone's best interest to finalise presentations, as much as possible, prior to this late stage. This makes for a better show.

Theme

Not all conferences have a theme but most have one key objective – the message that the brief provider wishes to be conveyed to the delegates attending. As such, you, your boss, colleague or client may like to consider creating a strap line for the conference. A strap line is normally the message of the conference. 'Keep an Eye on the Action', 'Believe It' and 'Ahead of the Rest' are all strap lines some of my clients have utilised.

There are design agencies that can innovate such strap lines and also create a logo for the occasion which can then be incorporated into a template PowerPoint slide for the conference presentations. Then again, this is quite a costly exercise and resource.

You may, therefore, have an in-house design department you can draw upon or failing that you may simply wish to sit round the table with the team and put your thinking caps on and let the creative juices flow – this is how many a conference team formalises their strap line.

Template slide

When the brief provider is happy with the designed strap line and they would like a template slide created, you may like to consider the production company producing the slide. Once innovated, each presenter can create their own slides by utilising the template incorporating the strap line, which will guarantee uniformity and continuity.

Top Tip Ticks:

The production company should be able to provide tips on how to most effectively put the conference presentations together, including the best picture and image formats, colours to use for text or background, minimum size fonts, suggested type face, maximum bullet points per slide, chart and video formations.

Logistics

Working hand in hand with event/conference content are the logistics. Similarly to visualising walking into a party, you need to visualise the conference itself from beginning to end. This will include visualising when and how the presenter takes to the stage? What will the stage look like? What will the delegates hear? What will the delegates see? Will an opening video sequence be shown. If so, will the production company have to produce and edit this? Will the presenter move around the stage or will he/she prefer to stand behind a lectern? Will the presenter wish to forward his/her own slides or will he/she require the production team to do this? Will he/she be reading from a script or working from cue cards? When inviting delegates up from the audience or changing over presenters, what will the audience hear (walk up music)? What will the audience see (name and title slides)? How many presenters will there be in total and how many presenters will be on stage at any one time? Will there be a *questions and answers* section which needs to be considered? If so, how many roving microphones would be needed? What about staffing for this? If there are a large number of delegates attending, would a live camera feed be helpful for picking up an image of the presenter and projecting onto the large projection screen? Or perhaps additional relay screens? What about recording the event?★ Is there a requirement to have an audio record of the conference or perhaps a video created to be circulated after the event?

Many, many questions but once you have undertaken the visualisation process, you and/or the brief provider can start to answer the questions this process has raised and in turn finalise an accurate brief of the level of support anticipated to be needed by the production company.

Clarification of what is visualised will raise questions and hopefully answers such as the need for: a lectern, autocue, lapel microphones, comfort monitors, cue light for lectern, music selection, live camera feed, recording of the event and any prop requirements.

Top Tip Tick:

Prior to any rehearsals being undertaken on site, try to arrange with the location for all the chairs to be placed in the room when the production company have finished set building. It always helps presenters to rehearse in a room set up for the right number of delegates so they can gain a feel of their audience size.

Don't forget to factor into the logistics placing some water on the stage – ensuring there are enough clean glasses for each presenter should there be more than one. Also, to make certain that some reserved signs have been created to place on seats should the presenters be gaining entry to the stage from the audience.

★ If the brief provider is considering having the conference filmed and videos duplicated, copyright issues will need to be taken into account. If duplicating and distributing to delegates, you may need to take advice regarding music utilised in the editing stages – music use is charged for on a time basis and if utilising a chart track, these costs can be extremely high. The best way of keeping costs down to the minimum is to utilise library music - the production company would guide you on this issue.

Running Order

When you have a good idea of the conference content, put your thoughts down on to paper i.e. create a Running Order. The Running Order is a live document, but it will eventually become a sub mini-itinerary, detailing the music to be played throughout, the particulars of the presenter(s), what he/she is talking about and clarification of the slides and video tapes utilised in sequential order. When this is as complete as you can make it, forward it to the production company who will, most certainly, place it into a workable format. The production team will then work from this one document during the show, having been constantly updated as the conference format is determined.

Do ensure that you confirm to the production company the final number of delegates attending and the number of presenters. This will provide a good all round feel and better understanding of the event.

Subsistence

When organising a conference or, indeed, an award ceremony, wherever a set is being utilised (including stage, light and sound) there will be a lot of kit and crew involved with setting up, running the show and striking.

Always establish with the production company the number of crew on site at any one time and make certain that they are taken care of by means of providing lunch, dinner and plenty of soft drinks, tea and coffee (especially during the load-in and striking period, as this is thirsty work).

Crew tend to like a good mixture of protein and carbohydrate as there is a great deal of manual work involved, so a healthy and nutritious buffet comprising of both hot and cold dishes, along with some jacket potatoes (and/or *chips* as the crew may also request) always go down very well.

Communication

So, your crew are well looked after, so are your event managers but it is very important that both teams strike up a good relationship as undoubtedly the smooth running of the event relies upon good communication between both parties.

As such, I find that it is best to allocate one senior event manager to be in communication with the Production Director or alike during the conference by means of a *talk back* system to keep abreast of whether the conference is running to time etc. Both 'under run' and 'over run' situations are frequent and it is essential that the location, via the event management team, are kept aware of timings to make sure that the event continues to operate smoothly when considering such aspects as providing refreshments, lunch or dinner to the delegates/guests at the appropriate time.

Badges

When delegates arrive, there is normally a requirement for a formal registration. At this registration, guests may be given registration badges and a delegate pack, so plenty of room will be needed. Remember to organise this area with the location.

Whoever is responsible for creating the guest list and registration badges, it is always best to ask the invitee what name they would like to have printed on their badge. For example someone called Rebecca may be known to her colleagues as Becky, so much better to have this name feature than her full forename. However, if the delegates are staying overnight, it is crucial to book their accommodation under their full name as it would appear on their passport or credit card.

Registration can take place in many forms. It truly does depend what your boss, colleague or client wish to do with the registration details after the event. If it is a matter of just checking who attended the conference, then a simple alphabetical list and registration badge may suffice. Alternatively, a computerised system may need to be considered so that data can be utilised subsequent to the conference.

Delegate Packs

Should there be a wish to provide attendees with Delegate Packs, the content of these packs vary. As a rule of thumb, they include the conference agenda whilst some also include printouts of the presentation slides, paper, pen and anything else relevant to the conference and the delegates attending. If there is a theme to the conference and if it is your responsibility to create the packs, be mindful to continue the theme throughout the body of the Delegate Pack, perhaps by utilising the conference strap line, colours and font.

Top Tip Tick:

If there are any overseas guests attending, it may be wise to check if they are fully conversant in English otherwise the engagement of the services of a personal translator or translator bureau to be set up within the conference room may be required.

If translators are being organised, don't forget to factor in their subsistence and accommodation. Should delegates be having a meal, most translators will need to sit with their designated person so remember, under these circumstances, to arrange for their food, to allocate for them to sit with the relevant guest and to feature on the table plan.

Award Ceremonies

If the brief provider is wishing to stage an award ceremony, most, if not all, of the details aforementioned relating to a conference should still apply as there is normally a 'set' involved and, indeed, a format to the ceremony. Then again, award ceremonies normally take place during or after a formal dinner. So when investigating suitable locations and capacities, rather than requesting Theatre style, the seating layout you will normally need to establish would be Banqueting (sitting at round tables) or Dinner Dance (allowing for a dance floor).

A few particular nuances to consider for award ceremonies, therefore, include:

Awards

One important aspect that tends to be left as a last minute thought is the awards table. Nothing looks worse than if great care has been taken to create a stunning set and just a 6ft trestle table and white linen cloth has been placed on stage to act as the awards table!

When discussing the set requirements with the selected production company, ensure that the awards table is given as much thought as the rest of the set. You can play your part by clarifying the size and number of awards/trophies that have to be displayed to safeguard that the table is large and sturdy enough for the requirements.

Top Tip Tick:

When considering the awards/trophies, always order (or factor these to be arranged) well in advance to make sure that enough time is available for engraving.

When considering logistics, remember to contemplate someone laying out and handing out the awards. You will be amazed how many people forget to do this.

Celebrity Host

Although not essential, a celebrity host can be a great asset to an award ceremony. There are many celebrities who will perform at *corporate* events and a reputable agency will provide a representation list of celebrities along with a guideline price for their services. (Locating a reputable agency is very much like securing a good supplier – utilise the same process as previously described.)

Regardless of who is selected, always make certain that you provide a comprehensive brief to the agent. The brief should give some background on the host company, the reason for the award ceremony and any insights and relevant information on the presenters/recipients that you feel may aid the compere.

Music

One of the most important aspects of an award ceremony is the music. 'Walk on' and 'walk off' music for both the presenters and the recipients of the awards will need to be chosen. Sometimes, music that is relevant to the person in question may wish to be featured or just that upbeat music is utilised.

I would advise that the music selection is contemplated well in advance. I find that throughout the year, if I hear a song with a good beat, I will earmark this for use at an event and, when relevant, propose its use - you will need to liaise with the production company who will also undoubtedly have some suggestions.

Photographer

Securing the right photographer is paramount for award ceremonies. When he/she is commissioned make certain that you have provided, well in advance, a Call Sheet for the photographer to work from, along with the final draft of the Running Order. A Call Sheet is a list of all the shots that either you or the brief provider would like the photographer to take.

With this in mind, when considering the layout of the room, discuss with the photographer, where he/she will need to be located. If the only space is on the floor but the stage is two feet high, sometimes the recipients can look a little 'squished' from having their photo taken at a slightly odd angle. The photographer may require to erect a backdrop within a roped off area, so work closely with him/her and the production company to ensure that the best results can be obtained. And, don't forget, the photographer may also need a power source.

Recipients

When considering the table plan, it is a good idea to place the recipients of the awards close to the stage. If securing follow spot operators, provide the production company with a floor plan which indicates where the recipients should be sitting. This will enable the follow spot operators to select guests from their tables and follow them to the stage, thus ensuring a more professional edge and well produced show.

Team Building

Objectives

Team Building is all about 'objectives' and establishing the objective is the most important clarification you will need to make. Most brief providers have an idea of what it is they would like to achieve from a team building event but others may need some help to get to grips with their burning issues. By talking through with your boss, colleague or client what the issues may be, this will help to determine the type of team building exercise you can suggest.

Take a moment to discuss what, if anything, this team has undertaken before and, indeed, the type of activities that were enjoyed and, conversely, the type of activities not so well received. This way you will be aware of the type of team building to avoid and also make sure that you do not replicate any event style previously undertaken.

Here we go with many questions… date, duration, location and number of participants are obviously important. Also, establishing exactly the type of event the brief provider visualises. Does he/she picture an outward bound type of event with few home comforts, sleeping out under the stars or up a mountain? Or, an activity in a controlled and dedicated safe environment where participants can undergo a series of team challenges which take the participants outside their normal comfort zone yet provide a positive learning experience?

Also, get to grips with those searching and probing questions such as… is the event to secure loyalty in the workforce and/or cement relationships between employee and employer? Is there a basic need to get teams to interact and communicate with each other? Perhaps the team event is an incentive award to encourage employees to meet targets or, perhaps, it is a reward day to thank staff for their commitment and achievement?

Either way, a team building experience is an excellent way of opening or establishing communication channels away from a work environment, through both relaxing and stimulating activities with the emphasis being on fun. Whatever the reason, once the key objective has been identified, then an event or event programme can be developed.

Once these questions have been asked and clarified, the answers will form the basis of your Event Brief Document.

Location Style

With regard to the location there are many to choose from, depending upon the level of team building the brief provider requires.

There are dedicated outward bound sites and team building locations to choose from; you can use the great outdoors or if suitable, you can utilise the grounds of a hotel/country retreat or venue.

Top Tip Tick:

'Exclusivity' needs should be queried. Some locations provide 'exclusivity' whilst others host many other groups, including children's, at the same time. Costs reflect accordingly but if going for the cheaper, non exclusive option, the group may (not always, but it is a risk) receive a less intensive and quality team building experience.

When considering the location, it is also important to establish a 'briefing' area (preferably under cover) large enough for the group. The most important aspect is to clarify the grounds available in which to undertake the team building – this is not such an issue if you are utilising a dedicated site.

Facilities

Participants don't normally mind 'roughing' it for an activity of this nature, indeed they are normally, one way or another, mentally prepared for it. However, if you want the group to all stay *happy bunnies*, give a thought to toilet facilities. If needs be, hire some portable toilets or if there are pleasant toilets within the vicinity of the activity make certain that they have ready access to these facilities.

Likewise, if the team building event takes place over a two day period and guests do not have the luxury of staying overnight in a hotel, consider hiring portable showers with HOT water. Again, participants don't mind roughing it, but they soon can get somewhat grumpy if they are wet, tired and cold! To maintain good morale – running hot water is a must. (I know a few Team Build suppliers who would disagree with me on this one but I always like to wear my 'corporate' hat and err on the side of some home comforts unless there is a specific reason for the lack of comfort where participants are perhaps undertaking a more hard core development programme.)

When participants undertake their initial briefing or are offered lunch and refreshments that have been arranged throughout the activity, contemplate weather cover. The weather cover will help provide relief should it be teeming down with rain or beaming down with sunshine.

Itinerary

You may feel that an in-depth itinerary for a team building exercise would be difficult to compile. However, as with any event there are always set parts to the day ie arrival of participants, H&S briefing, refreshments, team activities, lunch and prize giving, and all these aspects need to be timed and organised.

Flexibility is always required for the main activity time but all in all, you will still need to manage the *round robin*✶ process to ensure smooth transition. Creating an itinerary is a must if you wish the event to run well and to time.

Supplier Selection

Similar to a conference or award ceremony, the best way to make sure that you fulfil the specific brief and event objectives is to have the event content and format developed by a professional team build or leadership development company.

Many team build companies are run by ex military personnel whilst other companies are managed by instructors who have developed their competencies from a very different, psychology background. Whichever company you choose, team building activities should be undertaken under the supervision of a qualified instructor(s) and/or facilitator(s). It is also essential that the company you are suggesting is used to dealing with people/groups/companies similar to the clientele who are participating in the particular event.

It's *horses for courses* but as with selecting any other supplier; either yourself or where relevant the contracting party, should always check on the company's H&S policy and risk assessments for the event content they are proposing and that they provide proof of insurance. Your gut reaction will normally tell you if the company is right for the event, that and checking their credentials!

Top Tip Tick:

The kind of staffing ratio you should expect to receive is one instructor to eight participants. This will ensure that participants receive a concentrated development experience.

Depending upon the level of team building experience required, facilitators can take an active role. They can review all elements and draw out learning whilst providing helpful feedback on how individuals can achieve their goals and overcome any hurdles that they may have had to face during the team building experience. Taking this one step further, profiling tools can also be utilised which can provide a powerful insight to the recipient.

Theme

Can there be a theme? Absolutely. Is it essential? Absolutely not. A theme can add a fun element to the occasion and, as such, the activities that are undertaken can have a spin placed upon them to reflect

---

✶ Round Robin describes the formation in which a number of teams undertake a series of tasks. Team 1 may first be directed to Activity A whilst Team 2 would head for Activity B. After a while the teams would all rotate. Team 1 would then be directed to Activity B whilst Team 2 may be directed to undertake Activity A. Round Robin ensures that all teams undertake each activity within a set time frame.

accordingly but all team building events can be tailored to draw out learning and break down barriers, thus providing a great platform from which the team can develop. Most of all, in order to maximise learning potential, team building events should be fun, regardless of any theme being present.

Format

Generally, the group – which can be of all ages, either sex and level of fitness - will be split into teams which strengthen the shared experience and encourage communication. Teams undertake a number of challenges in rotation and this can include activities such as: high and low ropes course, initiative challenges, trust exercises, orienteering and classroom workshops when in a dedicated centre and/or incorporating the great outdoor challenges that nature provides such as rock climbing, abseiling, canoeing and traversing etc. These activities probe and highlight individuals' strengths and limits and explore ways/provide experiences through which they may learn about themselves and develop skills to achieve their objectives.

When securing the services of a good team build supplier, they will ensure that there is a variety of 'roles' for each type of activity. For example: an individual (who may have a fear of heights) can assist the group by providing rope safety in a climbing activity with two feet firmly on the ground. This is an essential role, as is verbally motivating team mates, so even if participants do have a fear of heights, they don't have to *climb* to be involved in a team building activity of this nature.

As a rule of thumb, be sure that the supplier incorporates cerebral challenges and workshops into a team building event to ensure that individuals who dislike or are unable to participate in physical activities have a task that they can excel at. For example, treasure hunts or navigation legs can be useful at linking widely-spaced activity stations together and allows/encourages participation.

Whatever type of team building experience, the learning should be relevant to the needs of the group or individual by relating issues and key learning points directly back to the workplace. The outcome will be that the team is actually working towards a common goal and the group is working towards an agreed vision and purpose.

Top Tip Tick:

On occasion the brief providers may have their own fears about the team building event i.e. they don't like heights, which they then try and mould into the proceedings. This can be a difficult situation as they are effectively trying to create their ideal event and potentially stop the rest of the group from having a go at an activity that some would excel at. A colleague of mine, who is the proprietor of a leadership development company, always says that you can never please every single person in the group with every single activity, so the best thing to do is to have a broad spectrum of activities in an attempt to cater for all needs. If you find yourself in a similar situation, although you may need to be tactful, do try to establish an overall event which will benefit the group rather than just the individual providing the brief.

Kit List

Team building or outward bound type activities have, unfortunately, received some bad press in the past and so some participants can understandably be a little apprehensive. As such, try to help to allay some of their fears – after finalising the content of a team building day, establish with the team build suppliers a Kit List suitable for the planned event and forward this to the participants. Do this well in advance to allow participants enough time to gather, borrow or purchase the kit suggested.

Participants who arrive with the right kit will be more mentally prepared for the event which contributes to the right kind of 'I can do this' attitude at the outset.

Competition

Ultimately, it's about all the teams working together for the greater good. Then again, depending upon the format of the team building event you are organising (although supporting individuals from within) teams may also wish to compete against each other. If this is the scenario, ask the instructors to complete a score sheet so a winning team can be announced at the end of the day.

Top Tip Tick:

Seek clarification from the team build company of the items they are providing. Items such as blindfolds, compasses, whistles, clipboards, pens, paper, stopwatches, back packs, air horns, score sheets and fun prizes are often utilised for team building purposes, but best to establish at the outset whether you need to take a trip down to a large toy store and an outdoor supplier or whether they do.

Instructors

The team build instructors should be personable and supportive as well as encouraging. They should be well presented (clean shaven) and wear a uniform to differentiate themselves from the group. They should be qualified for the tasks that they are instructing and be best able to engage individuals. Think about the age group, what age are the instructors? An eighteen year old could well come out of college with a fresh set of qualifications but may not have developed the maturity to interact appropriately with an adult group. When you meet your proposed team build suppliers, meet the instructors as well. Were they warm, friendly, 'corporate' and did they indeed appear to be knowledgeable? Did you like them, because if you did, the chances are that your boss, colleague or clients are going to like them too.

Top Tip Tick:

When embarking on a team building event, although not presently a legal requirement, I always suggest to my client that they should ask their participants to complete a confidential medical questionnaire. The completed forms can then be provided well in advance to the team build company so that they have prior warning of any medical and/or dietary conditions that they should be made aware of. Always ask the team build supplier to check if they are happy that the Questionnaire covers all the points that they need to know for their specific activity, or would like any details omitted, prior to sending to the relevant party.

Also make certain that the team build supplier offers a 'challenge by choice' policy which means that participants decide whether they are fit enough to undertake an activity or not – individuals are much better positioned to make an informed decision of this nature.

Activity Days

The very nature of an activity day means that it can be construed as a team building event. Sailing, rib riding, white water rafting, archery, crossbow – they all have an element of competition about them which can generate team spirit.

All the same pointers raised for team building should therefore be taken into account when organising an activity day and, as previously discussed, to guarantee the success of an activity day is dependant upon selecting the right supplier.

A few particular nuances to consider for activity days, therefore, include:

Alcohol

Some activities can not be undertaken if alcohol has been consumed. It is worth checking at the outset, on the conditions of the supplier's policy regarding alcohol and make sure that you disseminate this information to the brief provider.

Be especially careful if you are organising an overnight/two day event if alcohol has been present the night before as, if suffering from a hangover, with alcohol still in the system, the participants still may not be allowed to take part the next day. Where sailing in particular is concerned, the Skipper has full authority over the crew.

First Aid

When undertaking a team building or an activity day, always contemplate potential first aid requirements. Clarify in advance who the designated first aider will be on site and of their procedures should medical assistance be needed. Remember it is, under normal circumstances, the supplier's responsibility to administer first aid and to complete any Accident Log (s).

This is especially important as, should an accident occur, the inflicted person or persons in question presently have a number of years in which to make a claim.

Fun Prizes

Fun Prizes were mentioned as being part of a team building experience. Fun prizes relate even more to an activity. Whether there are two or twenty teams undertaking an activity, there will always be a competitive element. Make sure that the instructors take note of any outstanding achievements/individuals as well as any silly actions/comments which should be mentioned and rewarded at the end of the event.

The fun prize giving should always be undertaken in the right spirit… to reflect on the day's achievements and *fun* experienced.

Location Suitability

When selecting a Location, always check on any restrictions. For example, should there be a requirement to organise a beach BBQ with activities; best to check with the town's council first exactly what type of activities are allowed to be undertaken at sea and on sand, and what its policy is for music and alcohol. All councils differ.

Numbers

Remember, should the number of participants drop, then the price per head may increase, rather than decrease, due to fixed costs associated with activities.

Safety

When undertaking activities on the water such as sailing, you may like to ask whether a safety boat will accompany the group. I find safety boats are an excellent way of keeping tabs on the participants whilst at the same time enabling me, as the advance party, to check that everything is ready at the next stage of the event, without affecting the groups' activities. The safety boat can then also be potentially available for any individual that becomes unwell due to sea sickness or if anyone generally has to depart the main group during the activity.

Considerations

When undertaking any outdoor activity make sure, once the supplier has been selected, that you are made aware of any specific situations which may determine whether the event proceeds or, indeed, if individuals can take part. For example, if you wanted a group to go sailing, check at what stage an event could be cancelled should the weather become inclement. Likewise, check if there are any restrictions for any persons participating as rib rides do not normally allow for pregnant ladies to undertake the activity and can not accept individuals in excess of a certain weight. So, check first and make sure that this information is disseminated to the brief provider.

Although it is advisable to ensure that every participant completes a confidential medical questionnaire (and as you are collating information on behalf of the activity supplier, you have checked that the Questionnaire is fitting to the particular activity) you should, where relevant, and with the blessing of the activity supplier, make it known that some activities are strenuous and dangerous and require a certain level of fitness and good health. You may also like to include as standard, or amend according to the activity in question, specific questions such as whether participants can swim – this is important information for the supplier to know should the participants be undertaking water based activities.

Supplier's Terms and Conditions

Make sure that you read the supplier's terms and conditions thoroughly as for some activities a Damage Deposit can be requested. This Damage Deposit is normally associated with activities such as sailing and is required to be paid prior to the event. Should an incident occur, in accordance with the supplier's terms and conditions, then the amount to rectify the damage would be deducted from the deposit.

Press and Product Launches

Can you see a pattern emerging? When considering any event style, the step by step process should be followed and applied. In particular, you always need to contemplate the brief and the Brief Document(s), the location, event design and the supplier. Press and product launches are no different.

Objectives

A press and product launch will have a definite objective. The product can be a commodity, such as a *perfume*, whilst the launch can relate to a new release or soon to be released, *film* or alike. A press & product launch is an event hosted to promote either type of product and the press, among other guests, who could consist of retail outlet employees or end customers, are invited to attend the launch or promotion.

There may already be an advertising or marketing agency involved and the requirement could be just to 'organise' the event rather than come up with the event content/format. Either way, it is important to still understand the objectives in order to enable you to identify a location fitting to the launch and to create the right opportunities and emphasis throughout the event.

Your key aspects to clarify are quite simply: the product being launched, the demographics of the guests invited, the timings, preferred location style and the overall feel of the event.

Location Suitability

This is one of those events that are more often than not more suited to a venue rather than an hotel. In my opinion, it is important to link the location. The location is key.

For example, if the product was a *ying and yang* perfume, the event could be held in a Zen garden. If the product was a tank, then the function could be held in an army barracks or a venue that has military connections. If the product was a new species of flower then the occasion could be held in a magnificent conservatory.

One important point though, is to ensure that the location selected is easily accessible and has major forms of transport and road links close by – you want to eradicate as many hurdles as you can to guarantee that the guests can freely attend. At the same time, the aim should be to create a buzz about the event, encouraging invitees to accept the invitation and if, by utilising a slightly unique venue enables you to do this, then so be it…

Event Design

This is one of those examples where I feel that the selection of the location drives the format and décor of the event. Once a perfect location has been secured, then you can progress with the format of the event and then identify the best places to display the product and also to welcome the press and guests. Always ensure that, whatever is being promoted, it is given prominence at the function.

Depending upon the time of the event, make certain that there is plenty to eat and drink and if at all possible, link the food to the product. For example, if a Japanese car is being launched, then after considering the location such as a studio utilised to film a popular car programme, contemplate the food – such as sushi and general Japanese fayre, served with saki and alternatives for those guests who prefer more traditional drinks or non alcoholic beverages.

If involved with the launch of a film or TV programme, try to see the film or programme at a preview screening in order to get a real feel of the storyline. After obtaining clearance, take notes of anything of interest that you see such as: the locations utilised, foods that were eaten, drinks that were consumed, décor designed, entertainment that was featured etc. This is an excellent way to start the theming concept that may be required.

Dress Code

Take a moment to consider the time of day/evening – making sure that you have advised the brief provider that the dress code should reflect accordingly. If a drinks reception commences from 6.00pm, chances are that guests will have to come straight from work so they can't be expected to be dressed in cocktail wear if the timings don't allow for the guests to have the opportunity to change. So think about whether the emphasis should be on getting the guests to arrive at a specific time or whether it should also contemplate dress code which may or may not have bearing on the product being launched.

Top Tip Tick:

Depending upon the brief, you may or may not be required to design the invitation and/or press release. As an event organiser, normally this remit would fall upon the brief provider to contemplate and create either the content of the invite or a specialised document such as a press release. Nevertheless, just to explain what a press release is… A press release, designed to invite a member of the press to attend the launch of something specific, may include: a description of what the event is all about, details of the product being launched and contact information, as well as including key information similar to that you may expect on an invitation.

My colleague in the press industry stresses the importance of those involved in people hosting a Press & Product Launch identifying in advance the format each press guest requires releases to be sent in, i.e. word document with jpeg photos. Be careful, if attaching photos, that the file size is not too big. They hate that! (Max. 50KB per photo.)

Press releases should only be created by those experienced in the media field as they know how best to market to the press and invitees. As such, I tend to leave this to the professionals and focus on what I do best, and that is creating the actual event. You may like to consider doing the same.

Press & Guests

There are most certainly best days in the week on which to hold a press & product launch. If working on behalf of a marketing or PR agency, they will know the best month, day and even time in which to hold an event to maximise publicity potential for the desired target audience and will have considered this when providing you with the initial brief, should there be flexibility of the launch date.

Nonetheless, if you are not working hand in hand with a marketing or PR company and your boss, colleague or client is responsible for creating the invite list and determining the date and time of the event, then investigation will have to be undertaken. When it has been identified which media the brief provider wishes to invite, then whoever has been assigned to undertake the investigation should make contact and ask the press office or editor of the most suitable day and time to attend an event. They will all differ as they have different deadlines but you or the person assigned to the task will get an idea of dates to avoid with one particular day that may suit most, which would signify when best to hold the event.

When the date arrives, you may have considered the production of registration badges for ease of identification. A photographer is, of course, an absolute must which I am sure you or the brief provider would have fully contemplated. Gone are the days when all newspapers employed photographers who sat around just waiting to cover 'hot off the press' stories and attend events… these days, more often than not, freelancers are brought in on an adhoc basis. An editor friend recently informed me how much it is appreciated when there is a photographer at an event so he can draw upon his/her pictures. This is also good for your boss, colleague or client as this would enable full control of the photography rights.

A few words of warning…Press can be fickle. To keep them well on side, do make sure that the event starts and finishes on time. The press, in particular, will not thank you if you delay the commencement of an event for a few people who are running late – deadlines are deadlines, so run to time. One member of the press said that in particular he liked any formal, obvious, sales pitches kept short and sweet so he could gain the most out of the event by mingling with the guests and hosts. Perhaps you may like to take this into account when considering the format of the event, should this be your remit.

Top Tip Tick:

Best laid plans… Don't be surprised if a member of the press confirms his/her attendance and fails to show. Press coverage is very much determined on what happens to be taking place in the news on that day. If a big story breaks then they may not have the resources to send someone to the press event you are organising. However, trade press are slightly different and are not governed so much by current affairs.

The brief provider will undoubtedly be producing a secondary press release which covers the event and, should the above situation arise, I know of a few circumstances where the press have been thankful that they could still run the story by utilising the press release covering the event and photographs taken by the commissioned photographer.

Finally, when guests leave and if budget allows, don't forget to suggest the provision of goodybags. I once heard of an horrendous story where an event company, which shall remain nameless, produced goodybags for a beauty launch and filled them with products which included those of its client's competitors! Hmmm, I think they kind of missed the point of a goodybag as well as losing the contract. So, word to the wise, when creating the goodybags, be mindful that the gifts included reflect the profile and product being launched.

Family Fun Days

Everyone loves a good family fun day – that's the generic term actually as many companies like to stage fun days with 'family' not always being present at the event.

A fun day, regardless of whether a family is invited, is normally an outdoor activity and comprises an array of marquees, entertainment (including mechanical) and a central arena ready for displays or activities such as It's a Knockout. The activities embrace everything from inflatables to fairground rides, and stalls with plenty of things to do and to see, food, drink and lots of general fun and frolics.

Age Range

The most important element of a fun day is to establish the age range. If children are involved then obviously a proportion of the entertainment has to be geared to take little ones into account. If it is an adult only affair then a face painter or balloon artiste isn't going to cut much ice!

So the many questions asked revolve around the guests attending.

Location Selection

Fun days can take place in a multitude of locations: cricket pitches, grounds of an hotel, sports facility, farmer's field – anywhere where there is access to water and where the ground is reasonably level.

If, however, you as the event organiser are proposing motorised activities, this may limit suitable locations due to the damage that this particular activity can cause to the land and so this is one question that needs to be clarified when establishing the brief.

Regardless of the actual location, always bear in mind that it takes some considerable time to set up a family fun day. If you want to start the event at 09.00 in the morning, you will need to hire the land the day before and also it would be wise to pay for security to be on site over the evening/night period. (This would also result in costs being higher for the many suppliers as you would also, in some cases, have to provide overnight accommodation as well as paying for a two day hire.) The best solution would be to start the fun day from lunchtime onwards, thereby setting up the same day, which would help to keep costs down to the minimum.

Event Design

Ripe for a theme but again, not absolutely essential, as so much colour and attractiveness can be generated by the very nature of the activities that take place at a fun day.

If young children are invited, make certain that there are some childrens' entertainers and perhaps some kiddies' races in the main arena along with some fitting inflatables. If teenagers are expected to attend, inflatables such as giant human table football or participation activities such as It's a Knockout will always go down well. Adults are more likely to be happy with a beer/Pimms tent, comfortable chairs, a BBQ and adult quad biking or similar.

Top Tip Tick:

When considering the provision of alcohol, some activities prohibit guests' participation if alcohol has been consumed, so this is always worth due consideration when contemplating 'beer tents' or alike or, indeed, the selection of activities.

Format

When considering the layout of the event, be careful to arrange marquee capacity for the number of guests. I have mentioned before the importance of having wet weather provision for all guests – even if this means calculating that all guests can take cover within a multitude rather than just one marquee. Wet weather is a consideration but so, too, is hot weather. Marquee cover enables guests to take advantage of shade. When thinking of marquee cover also contemplate outdoor seating such as benches, along with parasols, which would also provide much needed shade in the hot weather and don't forget that some suppliers may need to be placed inside a marquee.

Top Tip Tick:

Although fun days would appear to be a low risk activity some of the entertainment that is normally provided on such a day can be deemed 'high risk' by insurers. It is, therefore, advisable to check with whoever is insuring the event whether they are prepared to cover all activities proposed. For example, some insurance companies believe 'bouncy castles' and 'bungee running' inflatables to be of high risk and will not cover these activities. Under these circumstances, you could always suggest to your boss, colleague or client to check with their Employers Liability insurance broker to see if they will cover this particular activity for this one off event.

Talking about insurance, you can obtain Wet Weather insurance so, if the weather is appalling, the event can be cancelled but this type of insurance cover does tend to be costly. Most fun days that I have organised go ahead regardless of the weather conditions and so I feel the best way forward is just to contemplate large enough marquees so all guests can take cover if needs be.

When creating an outdoor environment it is important to plot the marquees and activities on paper and to scale. Try not to spread everything out too far as you will lose impact and also atmosphere. It is always a good idea to create a focal point, so try creating a central arena out of colourful bunting – this is where displays can take place along with any children's races. If organising competitions which include races, make sure that prizes have been purchased otherwise you will have some disappointed children and, it has to be said, adults, to contend with. Also take into account that you will need a reasonably powerful PA system to make announcements and to play background music to help create the right atmosphere. One important thing – don't forget the portable toilets.

Finally, where multi activities are available, especially with different age ranges, a few bumps and bruises can arise. It is advisable to erect a dedicated first aid tent along with either a qualified first aider or medic to be on hand, where their role is to solely concentrate on any incidents that may arise throughout the day. (St John's Ambulance will also attend these type of events for a donation to their cause.)

Supplier Selection

As mentioned previously in this book, especially for outdoor events, choose suppliers carefully.

You can locate suppliers from the usual sources as previously detailed but if you want additional peace of mind, ensure that they are a member of an association pertaining to their industry. (See Helpful Contact Details.)

Absolutely check their credentials and references. As per the responsibilities outlined in Chapter 7, ensure that insurance cover and risk assessments are in place and if possible that the suppliers have undertaken corporate bookings before. Public and corporate events are very different and sometimes corporate events require a certain amount of diplomacy to be applied, therefore having suppliers with the right attitude is almost as important as securing suppliers with the right equipment!

One of the most important suppliers is the caterer. Again, check that they are used to providing outdoor catering and that they have the necessary chilled vehicle(s), the outdoor catering equipment and also the expertise to achieve quality catering whilst contending with restricted space, resources and facilities. The caterer could also potentially look after *all* the catering needs including tea, coffee, beer, Pimms, afternoon tea and BBQ/buffet.

Top Tip Tick:

If you are creating a Children's Crèche area, ensure that the suppliers are OFSTED regulated. Advise the contracting party to check and retain their Registration certificate on file or should practicalities determine, request a copy from the supplier, check and then forward a copy to the contracting party to also check and retain.

Help is at Hand

CHAPTER 9

Fifty Top Tip Ticks

Fifty Top Tip Ticks

Twenty-one years of planning events have led me to learn many a lesson; here are fifty of my Top Tip Ticks:

1

Ask a location if it has any anticipated or scheduled refurbishments taking place. You don't want any surprises when you arrive to set up. (This happened to me where I entered a hotel foyer in advance of an event and I couldn't help notice that there was something missing – namely the hotel's central staircase!)

2

When wishing to provisionally hold a fair number of bedrooms at an hotel that is not the main location of the event (overspill bedrooms) you may be asked to sign an Allocation Contract/Agreement. This document is not supposed to be binding but just ensure that when you read through the conditions of the contract that the hotel has personalised the document making it absolutely clear, should accommodation not be taken up, that no liability can be assigned to you, your boss, colleague or client.

3

Sometimes events attract gate-crashers. Be vigilant, as the person hosting the event will not be too happy if random people are seen drinking their beverages or eating their food. This circumstance has been known to arise, so diplomacy comes into play.

4

Although the suppliers will need to adhere to any H&S issues pertaining to their service provision, remember that you must also adhere. In particular, if you, your boss, colleague or client are providing any theming always check that whatever is being provided is fire proofed. If it is not fire proofed make sure that flame retardant spray is utilised.

5

Depending upon the nature of the event, the brief provider may wish you to hire the services of a security company. If you are working within a large location with lots of guests coming and going and if you have lap tops or equipment that are, on occasion, left unattended, visible security can provide a good deterrent and peace of mind. Likewise, if you are organising a large party, it is always advisable to have some 'corporate' style security on hand for the occasion where party revellers may get slightly out of hand.

6

Coaches – if you know of a good, reliable coach company keep hold of them with both hands and never let go! Always, always get drivers' mobile numbers so you can establish their whereabouts if necessary. Also plan to assign coach monitors to check people on and off the coach(es) and obtain their mobile telephone numbers too.

7

If guests are staying overnight, confirm if the location will charge for luggage to be taken to and from guests' rooms. If so, you need to factor this porterage element into your overall event costing or, if the brief provider chooses not to absorb this cost, you need to make sure that guests are informed prior to their arrival that they will each be responsible for their own porterage charge or taking their own luggage to their rooms.

8

Similarly, if a gift is to be placed into a guest's room, there is normally a charge per item for this service. Having left yourself, or the person assigned to the task, plenty of time to purchase the gifts, make certain that the location is given the items with clear instructions and in plenty of time of the event. Discuss with your conference and banqueting team the timings for delivery to the rooms.

9

Safeguard that you have fully contemplated luggage storage requirements. If the event that you are organising starts in the early morning but guests are staying overnight at alternative hotels, they may need somewhere to leave their luggage/bags so ample storage space will need to be arranged.

10

If you have a favourite caterer (or indeed a specific supplier) never assume that they will be allowed to provide their service within a location. Some locations have 'tied' caterers whereby clients are asked to select from their preferred suppliers list. Do, therefore, check with the location if there are any exceptions to the rule should you especially wish for a specific caterer or indeed any other specific supplier to undertake the role. Obviously, this aspect needs to be clarified prior to confirming the desired supplier or/and indeed location.

11

If there is a desire to utilise a more unusual venue or outdoor location, be precise as to the type of event to be staged and ask the location to confirm that it has the necessary licences in place. If not, then you, your boss, colleague, client or the venue may be able to apply for a licence but make these enquiries prior to confirming the location and also in plenty of time of the event.

12

If organising transportation – assume that there will be some guests who arrive late. So leave a responsible event manager behind at the departure location with access to transport such as a large vehicle or mini bus, just to collect stragglers - this will mean that the bulk of the guests are not held up. The event manager should be scheduled to wait for approximately thirty minutes after the scheduled departure time.

13

When calculating the amount of wine that you will need to organise for the guests, it is best to assume the calculation of five glasses of wine per bottle. Rule of thumb, you need to allow for an absolute minimum of half a bottle of wine per person during dinner.

On the whole you should calculate the wine consumption to be two-thirds white and one-third red. Generally more guests drink white wine than red, although it does ultimately depend upon the menu chosen and the fact that trends do change.

14

Remember to confirm to the location who will be the authorised signatories during the event. This should normally be the key event manager and the directors of the company hosting the event or, indeed, the host(s) themselves. This will help to keep control of the expenditure during the evening. Provide a specimen signature(s) for all authorised personnel - you don't want someone signing off copious amounts of Champagne to your name, do you?

15

Generally keep the location updated with how the numbers are progressing. If numbers significantly decrease, be mindful of the terms for securing the main room whilst, if numbers significantly increase, make reference to the location's floor plan just to check that you are happy with the numbers and how the guests will fit into the room. Either way keep the location updated.

16

You may wish for the guests who are staying overnight to pre-register. This basically saves time when checking in, as guests tend to only have to sign a card rather than complete the form in full and, on occasion, credit card swipes are not even required. Check with the location the information that they require to be supplied in advance, in order to arrange this service and make sure that you or the person responsible collates this information prior to forwarding any request for details to invitees – you don't want to waste time by having to go back to guests for one more piece of information that the location may require. Likewise, if guests are pre- registering or for larger groups of guests, the location may be happy to set up a dedicated check in area. Discuss this possibility with your conference and banqueting team at the desired location.

17

Toilets should be clean and pleasant wherever you are but it may come as no surprise that this is not always the case! If the toilets are, after inspection, not so great, see how you can improve the situation. It's amazing how much difference some nice colour coordinated hand towels, soap dispensers, smellies and flowers can make.

18

These days all key locations cater for special needs. When undertaking a site visit, check on the disabled facilities and make sure that you are familiar with all aspects so that any disabled guest(s) attending are not placed in insensitive situations.

If feasible or should circumstances allow, you may also like to check whether any guests are pregnant. Ensuring that there is somewhere for the ladies to sit (in a cool area if the weather is hot) along with taking into account their particular dietary needs is, at the very least, a considerate gesture.

19

If providing theming on a 'hire' basis, then you will need to be mindful when guests depart that any hired theming is not mistakenly taken. Many guests are of the opinion that they can take theming and normally they are quite right to do so and in a way it helps because there is less to clear up and dispose of but when it comes to hired theming, be vigilant. Courteous, but vigilant.

20

One task that is nearly always forgotten…remember to ask the brief provider what they wish the welcoming board to say at the location, should there be one.

21

Before confirming the location, check if any other events are scheduled to take place at the same time. It can be terribly off putting should you be organising a classic dinner party when an 18th Birthday celebration is also taking place in a function room close by. It is also advisable to check what time the other event(s) finishes, as this may differ greatly and have a negative impact on the proceedings.

22

When planning a conference or award ceremony make sure that you 'time' presentations. Most companies will, say, allow for a fifteen – twenty minute slot per presenter but there have been occasions where on the day/night their presentation takes just ten or indeed forty minutes. It is important to monitor each presentation in advance to make sure that the conference or awards will run to time, thus ensuring that aspects such as refreshments, lunch or dinner can also run to schedule.

23

Be aware that if the location allows confetti cannons then they may request an additional cleaning charge which can be hundreds of pounds. Check on costs first.

24

As the non smoking ban came into force within the UK in 2007, identify where guests can smoke during the course of the event. Make sure that there is ample directional signage indicating the designated smoking area(s) and that there are adequate ashtrays and weather protection in place.

25

Unless otherwise informed, clarify that all guests staying overnight will settle their own room extras upon departure. Make sure that you disseminate this information to the location and that you or the person allocated to the task of guest liaison make this clear to invitees in advance.

26

If there is a need to purchase something from a supplier, if suitable, enquire if payment can be made by credit card. (I once had to purchase thousands of pounds worth of world cup football tickets from a supplier that I was unfamiliar with and even though references were undertaken, this company disappeared with my client's money and no tickets materialised. I paid by credit card and as I didn't receive any goods, the credit card company refunded the money in full – it was a fantastic outcome – another grey hair to add to my head but phew, what a result!)

27

When creating the H&S/pointer details (H&S Announcement) which may be presented to the guests prior to the start of an event, suggest to the contracting party that a note should be added about mobile phones, reminding guests to turn them off during the event. There is nothing more embarrassing for a guest or off putting for a host to have a phone ring at an inopportune moment.

28

When considering the needs of guests who may be attending a day event which follows through to an evening occasion but they are not staying overnight at the location – contemplate hiring a number of bedrooms that guests can utilise in which to shower and change. Remember, however, to always request additional towels and toiletries along with an iron and ironing board.

29

During the organisation of the event, amendments to rooming lists will undoubtedly arise. Ensure that the initial document is utilised (renaming each edition) but highlight just the amends each time there is a revision. This way the location can accurately and quickly make the desired changes to their computerised system.

30

Should in-house staff be utilised to act as event managers, best to check whether these personnel will also be covered on the existing company insurance or whether the company hosting the event will have to take out additional insurance cover.

31

When arranging internal flights, book either direct through group bookings of the airlines themselves or utilise a travel agent who is ABTA and/or IATA bonded. (Many years ago, I organised a group to fly to Scotland over Christmas and I arranged tickets for them from a reputable travel agent… unfortunately, it transpired that the travel agent hadn't paid the airline for my client's tickets but had pocketed the money just before faxing over details that the franchised company had gone into receivership. Although the travel agency displayed the IATA logo in the window and on their letterhead, unfortunately they had long stopped paying for the bond. So, if in any doubt, check with the association just to see if a membership is still current.)

32

When arranging the printing of anything such as balloons, make certain that you are working from the most up to date company logo and get the powers that be to sign off the artwork. This could be a costly and embarrassing mistake should an out of date image be used in error.

33

If a great number of people are scheduled to register and if arranging for a dedicated check-in, it is a good idea to split the check-in tables into four alphabetical sections ie A-F, G-L, M-R and S-Z but before doing this, check on the guest list to make sure that surnames are equally distributed and amend the alphabetical split accordingly if necessary.

34

When securing activity suppliers, entertainers and DJ's just double check that they are coming to the event alone rather than bringing with them their friends, parents, dogs, children — you would be shocked how many people/animals can sometimes accompany a supplier.

35

If arranging a residential event and some overseas visitors will be attending, check with the location if they are able to prepare these particular guest rooms as a priority should they be arriving prior to the stated check in time. If at all possible, it is important for a guest who has been travelling for a long time to be able to gain access to their room upon arrival.

36

These days with Blackberry handsets, or their like, most delegates can easily keep in touch with their office - it is, however, best to pre-empt the situation and ask the location if they are able to arrange conference calls?

37

One word — fraternizing! Fraternizing between event managers, clients, crew and suppliers on an event is not always conducive to a harmonious working relationship and should be avoided if at all possible. Enough said.

38

On events, guests' personal belongings are not normally covered by insurance. It may be wise for the contracting party to point this out which may encourage guests to take increased care of their own belongings.

39

When organising an event for a small group, try to obtain photographs of each guest and create a 'Who's Who' sheet. This way you and/or the event team can match a face to a name and greet the guest personally which will make them feel very special and you to appear to be, oh so super efficient. This also works well if wishing to be able to identify any key personnel on a larger event.

40

Likewise, for smaller groups, if their event is taking place in a hotel or venue that has an in-house map, mark all the areas of the location that the guests will be utilising and arrange for these to be personally handed to the guests during check-in. It's these small, personal touches that make all the difference.

41

If a letter has not been sent to attendees prior to the event confirming important details, perhaps you could suggest that the brief provider considers a welcome letter to be placed in each bedroom should guests be staying overnight. The welcome letter could reiterate: timings, dress code, meet and greet places as well as clarifying check-out times and whether it is wished for guests to settle their room extras upon departure.

42

You will have generally measured different aspects during your site visit(s) but when specifically providing theming or props, always seek confirmation of the various dimensions. Also, measure the access to the location and the various doorways/corridors en route to the room(s) where they are being utilised, just to make sure that the props can actually get through the doors. (When I was a 'rookie' I hired a fabulous witch's cauldron for a Haunted theme but didn't consider the relevance of measuring the dimensions of the front door. The cauldron arrived but wouldn't go through the entrance so it was utilised as some impromptu arrival theming instead.)

43

If organising a VIP event, I always find it best to physically check the bedrooms assigned to those guests high on the pecking order list. This will guarantee that you remain confident the best rooms have been allocated to the right people but also provides the opportunity to make any last minute changes should you feel it right to do so prior to the guests' arrival.

44

When taking special dietary needs into account – double check with the location that wherever food is being served it has clearly indicated which dishes contain specified intolerances.

45

When considering alcohol, as a rule of thumb only soft drinks are usually served during lunch (unless solely organising a luncheon).

46

If planning part of the event off site – arrange for event management personnel to be sent in advance of the main party just to make sure that the location is all up to speed and ready for the guests' arrival.

47

If you have arranged transfers (including taxis and limousines) make certain that there is a dedicated person on duty as 'transfer' requests frequently change and in my experience, this can often become a full time duty.

48

When guests are checking out of their hotel rooms, I like to have a member of staff in the reception area to be available to answer any questions that may materialise. It's a shame if the guests leave feeling agitated over a silly incident during check-out when you or an event manager could have been there to make sure that everything flowed smoothly.

49

Request to see the location's 'table plan holder' – to ensure that the table plan will fit accordingly and when sorting place cards put them in 'table groups' and in order of seating for each table, this will help save time when the task of placing the cards on tables is undertaken.

50

If organising a dinner, make sure that you have previously arranged for a hands free microphone to be available for any impromptu speeches.

CHAPTER 10

The A–Z Survival Guide

The A–Z Survival Guide

This A–Z is your survival guide to becoming a proficient **event organiser** and *manager*. The guidelines are a combination of reiterated key points raised in previous chapters and some additional pointers for both organising events within the office environment and managing the event when on site at the location.

A is for AUTHORISATION & ATTITUDE

> **A is for Authorisation.** Never formally confirm any locations or suppliers without authorisation from the brief provider.

> *A is for Attitude. Attitude is everything if the event manager is to survive the strains of running an event. This means: enduring the long hours, appearing fresh faced as well as being mentally prepared.*

> *Positive attitude goes a very long way. Yes, you will be tired but it is very important that your boss, colleague, client or guests are never aware just how tired you are.*

> *Never fret, never run, act calm and those around you will remain calm as well. Problems do arise; the best way to address those problems is to find a solution – positive attitude.*

B is for BORROWED TIME & BANQUETING MANAGER

> **B is for Borrowed Time.** We always think that there is plenty of time to organise an event and before we know it, the event is upon us. So, try to organise everything as early as possible and work closely to your Benchmark Schedule.

> *B is for Banqueting Manager. These people are the mirror image of ourselves (well usually) they understand the business and they should be an expert when dealing with the ins and outs of their particular location. Get to know your Banqueting Manager and endeavour to strike up a good relationship as you will be working hand in hand with him/her during the event.*

C is for COSTINGS & CLOTHING

> **C is for Costings.** It is extremely important that your costings of the event are kept up to date to ensure that you work within the budget. Always make certain that all costs are consistent ie

plus VAT (if your company or your clients are VAT registered) to guarantee continuity and accuracy, and don't forget to add, where appropriate, any additional costs to your Extra Costs Sheet.

C is for Clothes. Think practical.

D is for DETERMINATION & DISCIPLINE

D is for Determination. Be determined to make this event the best event ever. Always adopt the 'that will do, will NEVER do' attitude and try to be as creative as you can when considering any theme for an event by utilising the many resources available to you. Go on. Strive for that WOW factor.

D is for Discipline. *It is important to apply self discipline. Where there is a copious amount of drink around it is very easy to accept a drink or two. When already feeling weary, alcohol only makes you feel more tired and it is not generally acceptable to drink in front of the guests.*

E is for EVENT BRIEF and ENERGIZE.

E is for Event Brief. Remember to establish the Event Brief at the outset. A clear brief will save you a great amount of time in the long run.

E is for Energize. *To keep yourself energized during an event, drinks lots and lots of water and eat bananas or any other suitable fruit.*

F is for FORESIGHT & FRIENDLY

F is for Foresight. If, when you first undertake a site visit, the room(s) in question looks bland, let your creativity flow and imagine what the room could look like - with a little foresight you may be on to a winner.

F is for Friendly. *No matter how tired, no matter how tiresome some guests can be, you must always, always be friendly.*

G is for GROOVE & GOD

G is for Groove. Get into the groove of the working week. Do not detract from your tasks and schedule of the day and never deviate from the organisational process.

G is for God. *I am afraid that 'He' will not be able to 'give you strength'; you need to find this within and with support, if applicable, from your fellow event team.*

H is for HAPPINESS & HELP

H is for Happiness. Happiness is definitely a ticked off list. Remember to highlight each and every duty when it is done.

H is for Help. *You are never alone. Any problems or last minute changes, share them with the location's banqueting manager or a trusted event manager. A problem shared is definitely a problem halved.*

I is for ITINERARY & INTELLIGENCE

I is for Itinerary. Keep your Itinerary open at all times. Add questions, input answers, change to statements but ensure that it is up to date at the close of each working day.

I is for Intelligence. When things don't go exactly to plan, just do your very best to rectify the situation and to the best of your abilities.

J is for JAUNTY & JOKING

J is for Jaunty. Remember throughout the step by step process that you don many a hat. Your 'guest' hat, your 'event organiser' hat, your 'creative' hat and not forgetting your 'environmental' hat.

J is for Joking. If you can see the funny side, even when you are tired, it will help to make light work. Try to keep a sense of humour; it really is a wonderful pick me up.

K is for KITTEN & KEEP IT CLOSE

K is for Kitten. Don't have a kitten - ensure invoices are paid on time and arrange for items such as 'awards' to be ordered well in advance. Keeping your working file and computer files in good order should help to keep to deadlines. You don't want to have to add to the stress.

K is for Keep it Close. Your itinerary should be kept close at all times. Never leave it unattended for anyone to pick up and read – the document is confidential.

L is for LISTS & LEARNING

L is for Lists. As well as working from your Benchmark Schedule and Itinerary, keep abreast of the duties on your overall To Do List and keep on adding tasks to do as and when you think of anything.

L is for Learning. Being an event manager is an ongoing learning experience. Always be ready to accept guidance and register guidance given. Every event you should learn something new and hopefully this will help to prepare you for the next time should a similar situation or problem arise.

M is for METHODICAL & MONEY

M is for Methodical. An event organiser has to be methodical in his/her approach. Tidy file, tidy desk, tidy mind.

M is for Money. Make sure that you keep on top of what is being spent and that the location's banqueting manager keeps you up to speed with the expenditure during the event itself.

N is for NOTES & NO SMOKING

N is for Notes. Never throw away any of your notes. You will be amazed how frequently you refer to them when checking how you calculated something or a decision came about. Place them at the back of your file in the Notes section.

N is for No Smoking. Seriously, smoking is a real thorn in the side of an event manager. Firstly, there is never any time to have a ciggie break and secondly, it really is not pleasant for a non smoking guest to smell cigarettes on the clothes, breath and fingers of an event manager.

O is for ORGANISATION & OPPORTUNITY

O is for Organisation. Organisation of the all important site visit to the location. (Don't forget to arrange for the production company and any relevant suppliers to attend with you, should there be a need.)

O is for Opportunity. If there is ever an opportunity to do so, just take a five minute break; to gather your thoughts, rest your feet and rehydrate.

P is for PROGRESS MEETING & POLITENESS

P is for Progress Meetings. Always schedule regular progress meetings during the organisational process. This is a time you can review the progress of the Benchmark Schedule and to discuss any issues.

P is for Politeness. Even if guests are the worst for wear from drink, you must always, always be polite.

Q is for QUESTION & QUICK

Q is for Question. Ask lots of them.

Q is for Quick. Although it is very important to look smart, you do not have to be the 'beau / belle of the ball'. It becomes an art; taking a shower, freshening up your hair, applying new make-up (ladies of course) dressing in different clothes and all in twenty minutes. It does, nonetheless, have to be achieved as it is far more important to be on site before the guests arrive rather than attending late because the event management were taking time to glam up. So be quick.

R is for REPLENISH & RELATIONSHIPS

R is for Replenish. Give yourself plenty of time to replenish your Tool Box, and ensure that you have everything that you could potentially need for the event.

R is for Relationships. Take the time to build upon relationships when managing an event: be that with your fellow event managers, suppliers or location staff. You never know when you will need their help again or when your paths will cross.

S is for SHARE and SHARE ALIKE & STAMINA.

S is for Share and Share Alike. When considering on site duties for all the team, share the work load as you will all be in this together.

S is for Stamina. You need lots of this to get you through the management of an event.

T is for TERMS and CONDITIONS & TIME MANAGEMENT

T is for Terms and Conditions. Take time to read the fine print. If there is a clause that you or your boss, colleague or client do not agree with, then raise the issue and negotiate on that particular clause.

T is for Time Management. Take responsibility for yourself. No matter how tired you are, if you have to wake at a certain time, take responsibility to do so. Don't let the side down.

U is for UNDERWRITING & UMBRELLA

U is for Underwriting. You must ensure that each supplier underwrites to abide by H&S regulations pertaining to their service provision.

U is for Umbrella. *Not all functions are in a cosy environment; sometimes they are outside, sometimes in the rain. Think ahead… warm clothes and dress to keep yourself dry.*

V is for VITALITY & VICTORY

V is for Vitality. If the event is taking place over a two – three day period and you want event managers to be full of vitality for the duration, do ensure that you factor in more event management personnel than you would normally consider for a one day event. Additional breaks are needed as the pressure remains consistent over a longer period.

V is for Victory. *Hopefully, the event will have run smoothly and you can feel victorious that all your hard work has paid off.*

W is for WRITING & WARDROBE

W is for Writing. Always confirm details in writing.

W is for Wardrobe. *Within an event manager's wardrobe should be: trainers, a warm fleece, comfortable shoes, black trousers and a black dress.*

X is for X-RAY VISION & 'X' RATED

X is for X-Ray Vision. When organising the event, we all hope that we have considered everything there is to be considered and X Ray Vision would be one of those remarkable powers – by checking the Ultimate Tick List, this should provide some reassurance that you will have considered all things that there are to consider.

X is for 'X' Rated. *Sometimes, as event managers, we witness things that are confidential. Keep it that way.*

Y is for YIPPEE & YAWNING

Y is for Yippee. 'Yippee'. Another tick off the list when you have secured all the entertainers and suppliers.

Y is for Yawning. *Yep, you will have to stifle many a yawn as the event gets underway. Yawn to your heart's content within the confines of your production office but never in front of the guests.*

Z is for A- Z GUIDE & ZZZZZ

Z is for the A- Z Guide. Your complete A – Z guide to the event itself; your bible, your ITINERARY. The itinerary details every aspect of the job and of the event management duties. When complete, remember to forward by email to all key personnel and print out a copy for everyone.

Z is for Zzzzz. After the event has finished and when everything has been cleared, you will be able to sleep very soundly in your bed and take a very well earned long sleep.

CHAPTER 11

Your Tool Box

Your Tool Box

Every event organiser should have a tool box; I call mine my 'Bits and Pieces' box.

My Bits and Pieces box is a trolley that has a deep compartment at the bottom, a large middle compartment, top tray and sliding units.

I quite literally take it to every event, no matter the type of function I am managing, as I never know what I will need... I do, however, supplement the contents depending upon the event requirement but the basics include:

Bottom

- Rubber gloves
- Fire-retardant spray
- Polish and duster
- Disinfectant wipes
- Absorbent cloths
- Bin bags
- Extension lead
- Three-way plug
- Hammer
- Pliers
- Screwdriver
- Air horn
- Spare raffle tickets
- Spare CDs
- Umbrella
- Clipboard x 2

Middle Compartment

- String
- White Tac
- Cat gut

- Velcro strips
- Scissors
- Plastic ties (different sizes)
- Sticky pads (with loop hole for cat gut)
- Sticky pad squares (sticky both sides)

Top Tray

- Stapler
- Highlighter pens
- Post Its
- Pens/Pencils
- Glue
- Sellotape
- Ruler
- Calculator
- Whistle
- Stop watch
- Hole punch
- Camera and charger
- Spare place cards
- Sticky labels
- Tape measure

Sliding Units

- Paperclips
- Spare staples
- Drawing pins
- Pins
- Rubber bands
- Tags

CHAPTER 12

The Ultimate Tick List

The Ultimate Tick List

The following details have been compiled to create an Ultimate Tick List. Although loosely based on the format of this book, the tasks are not listed in strict sequential organisational/process order as it has been created to act as a 'double checker'. (Firstly, for the purpose of finalising the tasks to feature on the Benchmark Schedule, and secondly, to ensure that everything has been considered at the time of finalising the organisation phase.) Therefore, for ease, the tasks are, in the main, listed randomly but *grouped* (where possible) by category.

This tick list is not exhaustive but it does, in my opinion, include all the key aspects that a proficient event organiser should consider (albeit some tasks may be assigned to alternative parties). The list takes into account all types of events so you will need to omit those that are not relevant to the particular style function you are organising. This list has been compiled for use up to the time of going on site. As you continue to organise events and gain experience in the field, you may like to add some of your own reminders to the list.

Administration

Identified the Event Brief	☐
Created the Event Brief document	☐
Undertaken progress meetings (to gain initial agreement of brief, discuss elements included within budget and potential/preferred location(s), Benchmark Schedule and theme ideas)	☐
Location(s) considered	☐
Potential locations identified and sourced (A & B list created)	☐
Venue Find Agency sourced	☐
Created a Location Brief (considered the specific event style, requirement inc whether exclusivity is wanted and set up period required)	☐
Location(s) held on provisional basis	☐
Received quotes in writing from location(s) (inc. or exc. VAT)	☐
Negotiated on costs	☐
Established agency commission (if applicable)	☐
Opened Event Organiser's File	☐

Considered administrative methods (sustainable event)	☐
Inserted all necessary documents i.e. To Do List and Extra Costs Sheet	☐
Utilised the To Do List and Extra Costs Sheet	☐
Visualisation process undertaken	☐
Guideline Event Costing created (E&OE added to spreadsheet)	☐
Event elements identified (within budget)	☐
Corporate packs obtained/photos taken from location	☐
Full contact details at location established	☐
Site visit arranged at location inc overnight if applicable – location's policy on site visit expenses established	☐
Site visit(s) undertaken (for viewing, theming and logistical purposes)	☐
Initial site visit findings fully contemplated	☐
Guideline Event Costing updated incorporating location costs – costs excluding VAT (inc. set up period/room hire)	☐
Formal authorisation to proceed gained	☐
Location formally confirmed	☐
Confirmed set up period required to location	☐
Rooming list forwarded (pecking order)	☐
Received Contract from location	☐
Terms and Conditions contemplated and actioned	☐
Location Contract exchanged	☐
On site production meeting arranged	☐
Dilapidation tour arranged	☐
Released alternative locations on provisional hold	☐
Provisionally held 'overspill' accommodation (if necessary)	☐
Allocation Contract raised, checked and authorised	☐
Payment and cancellation terms established and scheduled	☐
Invoices scheduled for payment and paid	☐

Security Deposit raised	☐
Innovated Itinerary	☐
Innovated Benchmark Schedule (assigned duties, allocated for holidays and updated where necessary)	☐
Innovated a Theme ideas list	☐
Event Costing updated and finalised	☐
Amendments to proposal undertaken – brief provider informed of responsibility should amends be to the detriment of event	☐
Read through the Ultimate Tick List to double check all aspects have been assigned/organised	☐
Completed the Itinerary	☐
Circulated the Itinerary to the location, suppliers (where applicable) and event managers	☐
Printed out hard copies of Itinerary	☐
Pulled together key info documents such as rooming list, guest list, table plan, contact list and blank paper	☐
Itineraries bound	☐
Placed key documents on to disc or memory stick	☐
Created ID badges for suppliers, crew and event managers	☐
Ordered radios, holsters, covert earpieces and spare batteries	☐
Checked on any channels to avoid for radio usage	☐
Sourced plastic crates/boxes with lids for packing purposes	☐
Created tick list, laid out and packed aspects to take to the event: laptop, itineraries, memory stick, reusable ID badges, risk assessment forms (if relevant), insurance policy details (if applic) H&S form (if relevant) Accident Log (if relevant) radios and charger, mobile phone, tool box, print and design material, spare place cards and pen	☐

Location

Clarified that the location has the necessary licence for the event requirement	☐
Complimentary upgrades agreed	☐
Confirmed if any refurbishments are planned	☐
Checked on any general restrictions/code of conduct applicable	☐
Confirmed any special touches free of charge	☐
Confirmed if any other events are taking place, their nature and endex time	☐
Established if 'preferred' suppliers exist i.e. tied caterers have to be used	☐
Minimum and maximum numbers established	☐
Confirmed maximum capacity in layout required	☐
Checked on dimensions of tables	☐
Location clarified table/layout configuration based on desired numbers	☐
Checked and viewed table and table number holders	☐
Location provided floor plan(s) of configuration	☐
Confirmed if any function layout plans are required to be submitted to location (H&S)	☐
Forwarded any relevant Risk Assessments to location	☐
Discussed sustainable event processes in place/how best to implement	☐
Confirmed date and times of regular fire alarm checks	☐
Confirmed how many refreshment breaks are included in DDR	☐
Checked of any restrictions such as candles, balloons, smoke, pyros and confetti	☐
Checked if any charge for clearing confetti	☐
Checked if smoke alarm can be isolated	☐
Air conditioning status clarified	☐
Checked on mobile phone signals	☐
Checked on conference call facilities	☐

Checked on outside land line and broadband facilities including WIFI capability (including ISDN and broadband in main function room)	☐
Confirmed suitable area for registration	☐
Additional function rooms secured (for production office, suppliers/crew eating/changing/work rooms, breakout rooms etc.	☐
Arranged cool work room for florist with access to water if needed	☐
Furniture requirement/layout confirmed for function rooms	☐
Arranged water and fruit for the production office	☐
Established if location maps are available (internal layout)	☐
Checked if early check-in can be arranged for guests arriving early/travelling	☐
Confirmed if complimentary newspapers are provided (for overnight guests)	☐
Checked on business facilities and costs	☐
Checked on mini bar status	☐
Checked on dress code for all areas	☐
Final numbers confirmed	☐
Final rooming list provided for guests	☐
Confirmation regarding payment of room extras	☐
Checked on prices for porterage and confirmed if required	☐
Checked on prices for room drops and confirmed if required	☐
Considered if pre-registration is required (if so informed location)	☐
Requested clarification of the information that the location required for pre registration	☐
Considered if dedicated check-in is required (if so informed location)	☐
Confirmed situation of dedicated check-in	☐
Food and drink requirements considered throughout	☐
Clarified if location will serve one set menu or two dishes per menu	☐
Vegetarian options considered	☐
Timings for serving of food and drinks confirmed to location	☐
Serving process confirmed (for canapés, drinks and wine)	☐

Checked on layout of dining tables (i.e. no coffee cups)	☐
Menu and wine tasting undertaken	☐
Drinks tariff requested and forwarded by location	☐
Corkage charges confirmed (if applicable)	☐
Menu and wine confirmed	☐
Arrangements made to have menu (if buffet) detailing ingredients	☐
Special dietary needs confirmed (for guests, suppliers and event managers)	☐
Identified if there are any special rates for management and crew (dinner, lunch, refreshments and bed and breakfast)	☐
Considered most cost effective subsistence for personnel, suppliers and event managers working at the event	☐
Accommodation arranged for suppliers, crew and event managers	☐
Identified if a special rate for B&B can be secured for guests attending	☐
Identified the need for a stage, dance floor, sound and lighting (checked on whether location has any/costs)	☐
Microphone arranged within lunch/dinner setting	☐
Confirmed if any independent sound system(s) is available in areas being utilised (if so what format)	☐
Identified open air locations for refreshment breaks and smoking	☐
Clarified if directional signs are allowed in public places and any restrictions (i.e. not on walls)	☐
Confirmed with location how many directional sign holders it has and of their specification	☐
Checked the toilets to see if any upgrading needed/allowed – actioned	☐
Organised storage for non residents luggage	☐
Organised changing room(s) – with iron/board and mirror along with additional toiletries and towels	☐
Authorised signatories confirmed and sample signatures forwarded	☐
Clarification sought of the timeline and layout of the final bill/invoice	☐
Established when the function room/location needs to be clear	☐

Guests

Contemplated type of guests attending and ensured format and entertainment suitable for attendees	☐
Requested notification of any special dietary needs including allergies, phobias, full name as appears on passport and the name they would like to appear on registration badge	☐
Requested confirmation of any disabilities and informed the location	☐
Sought confirmation of any pregnant ladies attending and made any suitable arrangements	☐
Obtained head and shoulder photographs of all guests attending and created a photo registration sheet. (For small groups or for key personnel attending a large function.)	☐

Misc Tasks

Teaser considered	☐
Wording considered for invite	☐
Logo use authorised	☐
Identified transport links i.e. tube, roads, airport and train	☐
Obtained map and directions (if not in conference pack)	☐
Personalised covering letter (accompanying invites) contemplated and sent	☐
Invitee list drawn up (if applicable)	☐
Teaser and invitations sent out	☐
RSVP's collated	☐
Checked surnames fall into A-F, G-L, M-R and S-Z categories	☐
Directional signs considered (size and number)	☐
Menu details forwarded to printers	☐

Table plan considered and drafted (2 or 3 types)	☐
Place card details drafted and forwarded	☐
Welcome letter drafted and printed	☐
Delegate Pack contents contemplated and actioned	☐
Transportation considered and organised (coaches, taxis, flights and limos for guests)	☐
Mobile contact numbers requested and received from coach drivers	☐
Coach monitors assigned	☐
Mobile numbers for monitors requested and received	☐
For any flights booked, ensured that arranged through a bonafide ABTA or IATA bonded agent	☐
Checked if car parking is required and facilities available (for cars and vans)	☐
Negotiated on parking rates and reserved places if possible	☐
Contemplated the need for van hire and arranged accordingly	☐
Forwarded car/van details and of their arrival/departure times to location	☐
Considered contracting a H&S adviser (pre production and on site)	☐
Secured H&S Adviser and confirmed requirements if needs be (checked NEBOSH accredited, public liability and professional indemnity insurance)	☐
Considered security and contracting where necessary	☐
Sourced and confirmed a photographer and or cameraman (also checked on what facilities needed)	☐
Call sheet initiated and sent to photographer/cameraman	☐
Arrival time of boss, colleague or client confirmed	☐
Registration badging contemplated and details confirmed to supplier	☐
Considered if computerised registration system needed (if so, sourced)	☐
Considered the wording for the notice board and confirmed to location	☐
Secured alternative caterers (if not tied at the location or outdoor supplier needed)	☐
Considered the music requirement throughout	☐
Purchased any music CD's as required	☐
Checked if cake is required (for Birthday or Anniversary)	☐
Clarified if any flower bouquets are required as gifts/thank you	☐
Arranged any misc. insurance requirements	☐

Contemplated if any raffle taking place and, if so, arranged raffle tickets (if responsible to do so)	☐
Misc. prizes, awards, trophies, gifts for rooms and goodybags contemplated and actioned	☐
Engraving for awards and trophies arranged	☐
Checked through the Tool Box, and replenished where necessary	☐
Recycling bin(s) arranged/sourced	☐
Rubbish collection and disposal considered/arranged (on site & pre prod)	☐

Theming

Theming concept considered	☐
Examined location's colour scheme, crockery, chairs, napery and crockery	☐
Theming research undertaken (films, books and internet etc)	☐
Theming thoughts applied throughout (teaser/invites – to end of event)	☐
Theming contemplated; in particular, for food and drink	☐
Themed clothing for all staffing considered and actioned	☐
Contemplated if anything needed fire proofing (if so actioned)	☐
Confirmed measurements of theming aspect and load in/entrance/doorways leading to location being utilised to ensure that theming will fit	☐
Considered and organised any misc theming including:	☐
• Personalised pop-up or landscape banners	☐
• Ropes and stands	☐
• Entrance carpet(s)	☐
• Flame burners	☐
• Helium balloons (and/or balloon drop)	☐
• Inflatable props	☐
• Themed props and backdrops	☐
• Flags and swags	☐

• Swish curtain(s)	☐
• Floral décor (pedestal, occasional table arrangements and table Centres)	☐
• Music	☐
• Atmospheric lighting and music (including smoke)	☐
• Chair covers, linen, crockery and glassware (inc. charger plates and coloured goblets)	☐
• Bespoke theming	☐
• Coloured dance floor	☐
• Ice sculpture	☐
• Special effect projections and waterscreens	☐
• Pyrotechnic displays inc confetti cannons	☐
• Champagne & chocolate fountains	☐
• Water sculptures	☐
• Cocktail shaking	☐
• Cookery school	☐
• Wine tasting	☐
Animal enhancement	☐
Entertainment contemplated and organised (pre dinner drinks, dinner and post dinner) Such as:	☐
• MC	☐
• Close hand magician	☐
• Caricaturist	☐
• Live music (string quartet, Caribbean band, accordionist/violinist, orchestra etc)	☐
• Band	☐
• Dancers such as Tango, Can Can girls, Salsa or ballroom demonstration	☐

• DJ	☐
• Casino and poker	☐
• Staging, lighting, sound, star cloth etc	☐
• Alternative entertainment	☐
• After dinner speakers	☐
• Cabaret acts	☐
• Stilt walkers	☐
• Lookalikes	☐
• Opera performers	☐
• Make up artistes	☐
• Mobile massagers	☐
• Mind readers, pickpockets and escape artistes	☐
• Tribute acts	☐
• Paparazzi	☐
• Stunt shows	☐
• Contortionists	☐
• Theatre acts (inc murder mystery and game shows)	☐
• Mime artistes	☐
• Circus performers	☐
• Games (air hockey, pool and pinball etc)	☐
• Funfair rides	☐
• Pot spinning	☐
• Fun tattooists	☐
• Giant Scalextric	☐
• Human artistry (inc acrobatics, fire eaters, human robots, statues, jugglers and trapeze)	☐
• Impersonator	☐
• Firework show	☐
• Adornments or gifts for the guests	☐

Print and Design

Teaser produced	☐
Invitations designed and printed	☐
Directional signs printed	☐
Menu cards produced	☐
Table names designed and printed	☐
Table plan produced	☐
Place cards produced	☐
Delegate packs printed	☐
Registration badging printed	☐

Suppliers

(i.e. entertainers, themers, production company/personnel, team build company/personnel, activity providers and misc. suppliers)

Suppliers sourced	☐
References undertaken	☐
Credentials provided and checked	☐
Discussed sustainable event processes in place (if any) and how best to implement	☐
Suppliers met or services listened to/viewed (if applicable)	☐
Quote(s) received in writing (inc. or exc. VAT)	☐
Checked to ensure if 'back up' equipment provided within quote	☐
Negotiated on costs	☐
All details formally confirmed including: time and duration of performance, location details, specific requests and confirmations, dress code, agreed fee and payment terms, etiquette and set up period/load out times	☐

Agreement/Contract issued and or exchanged	☐
Terms and Conditions received and considered	☐
Any Rider taken into consideration	☐
Insurance details supplied by Supplier	☐
Suppliers confirmed they will comply with H&S pertaining to their provision	☐
Risk Assessment provided by Supplier	☐
Paid by credit card (where applicable)	☐
Suppliers undertaken site visit (where appropriate)	☐
Key dates established and added to Benchmark Schedule for action	☐
Dietary needs clarified by suppliers	☐
Number of personnel on site clarified by suppliers	☐
Names provided for accommodation by suppliers (if applicable)	☐
Mobile numbers confirmed	☐
Vehicle type and registration requested (if necessary)	☐

Personnel

(*internal* personnel helping to organise and attending the event)

Organisational duties assigned	☐
Progress meetings scheduled/undertaken	☐
Clarified accommodation requirements	☐
Requested and received any dietary requirements or special needs	☐
If helping on site and acting as event managers; candidates considered prior to selection (ensuring suitable for duties and stamina required for event management)	☐

Event Managers

Event managers sourced	☐
Considered and assigned on site management duties	☐
Discussed sustainable event policy for event (inc. in-house personnel)	☐
Considered event managers dress code (set up and event)	☐
Event managers confirmed (date, duties, fee, expenses, times, location, terms, dress code and payment terms)	☐
Mobile numbers requested and received	☐
Received confirmation from event manager in writing	☐
Requested confirmation of their employment status ie self employed or employed	☐
Enquired if they have their own Public Liability insurance cover if not, arranged (including in-house personnel)	☐
Sourced outdoor clothing if required	☐

Logistics

All event logistics contemplated	☐
• Guest's view	☐
• Event Organiser's view	☐
• Creative view	☐
• Environmental view (sustainable event)	☐
• Event view (i.e. what is needed to complete logistical task – White Tac for erecting directional signs etc)	☐
Sustainability measures put in place(organiser/location and suppliers)	☐
Disabled access considered	☐

Required number of event management calculated	☐
Cloakroom requirements contemplated and actioned (facilities checked and prices established)	☐
Calculated subsistence for all on site personnel	☐
Considered transportation for event management and personnel	☐
Considered and arranged overnight accommodation for on site personnel	☐
Considered the need for any petty cash on site (if so, arranged along with tip)	☐

Nuances – Conferences/Award Ceremonies

Checked on: ceiling height, pillar status, load in, blackout facilities and power capability during initial site visit	☐
Liaised with location's technician re power	☐
Clarification of whether front or back projection is required	☐
Contemplated set requirements (inc. stage and speaker support material)	☐
Seating style considered	☐
Maximum capacity in seating and projection style confirmed by location	☐
Breakout rooms and equipment needed in each contemplated	☐
Preview and rehearsals scheduled	☐
Considered adequate set up and rehearsal time	☐
Arranged time with location for chairs to be set out for rehearsal	☐
Contemplated conference/award content and material format	☐
Contemplated the need for any translators or translator bureaux	☐
Arranged translator's accommodation, subsistence and added to table plan if sitting with a guest	☐

Created a Production Brief for production company	☐
Secured services of production company	☐
Production company provided tips for presentation creation	☐
Visualised the conference beginning to end	☐
Contemplated: script writer, autocue, guest speakers, motivational speaker, audience participation, material (ie video production) MC, celebrity host, smoke & pyros, PA system(s), lapel and hand held radio mic requirements, lectern, confetti canons, props, cue light, script or cue cards, comfort monitors, Q&A, live camera feed, follow spots and recording of event (audio and video)	☐
Production company clarified music copyright	☐
Briefed celebrity host(s) on company, presenters and guests	☐
Strap line considered and confirmed to production company	☐
Template PowerPoint slide created	☐
PowerPoint presentations finalised (including name/title slides)	☐
Material/Script deadline established and informed to brief provider	☐
Considered walk *in*, *up* and *out* music	☐
All music required fully contemplated and sourced	☐
Final numbers confirmed to supplier (presenters and guests)	☐
Location of recipients plotted on seating plan and given to production company	☐
Conference or awards Running Order contemplated and forwarded to production company	☐
Personnel logistics contemplated including who is laying out/handing out awards, microphones etc	☐
Event Manager assigned to liaise with Production Director	☐
Talk back facilities organised (between Event Manager and Production)	☐
Water and glasses arranged to be placed onto stage	☐
Reserved signs created	☐
Confirmed number and dimensions of awards to production company to arrange suitable awards table	☐

Team Building and Activity Days

Team building objectives considered	☐
Consideration given to any particular theme required	☐
Identified if team build/leadership development company offer a 'challenge by choice' policy	☐
Instructors met face to face (suitability assessed)	☐
Instructor/facilitator: participant ratio established	☐
Secured services of a team build/leadership development company/team	☐
Event format clarified (ensuring broad range of activities for all)	☐
Logistics fully considered (inc. timings for round robin)	☐
Sufficient soft drinks and subsistence arranged	☐
Profiling tools required (if so arranged)	☐
Weather contingency contemplated and arranged	☐
Group divided into teams	☐
Confidential Medical Questionnaire forwarded to supplier for authorisation	☐
Confidential Medical Questionnaire amended if directed	☐
Confidential Medical Questionnaire forwarded to boss, colleague or client, completed and returned to supplier	☐
Checked for any non swimmers (if relevant)	☐
Kit List identified and authorised by supplier and forwarded to participants	☐
Safety boat arranged for water based activities	☐
Checked on any specific situations resulting in postponement of event or circumstances where guests could not participate	☐
Checked on alcohol policy of suppliers	☐
Checked on age and fitness policies	☐

Policy information disseminated to brief provider	☐
First aid contemplated	☐
Portable toilets and showers organised if needed	☐
Equipment arranged or purchased ie:	☐
• Blindfolds	☐
• Compasses/whistles	☐
• Clipboards, pens and papers	☐
• Stopwatches	☐
• Backpacks	☐
• Air horns	☐
• Score sheets	☐
• Fun prizes	☐

Press and Product Launches

Objectives considered	☐
Investigated the product and considered format of event to reflect accordingly	☐
Contemplated a fitting theme and incorporate throughout	☐
Established best date/time for event to take place bearing invitees in mind	☐
Established who is writing and actioning the Press Release	☐

(Family) Fun Days

Fun day objectives considered (inc. if children are attending)	☐
Considered if a theme should apply	☐
Secured the services of outdoor suppliers (such as inflatables, mechanical entertainment, stalls and fairground, It's a Knockout etc)	☐
Checked crèche suppliers are registered with OFSTED and retained copy of Registration certificate. (Advised contracting party to check and retain on file or requested a copy from supplier, checked and then forwarded to contracting party)	☐

Checked on alcohol restrictions with suppliers	☐
Sourced outdoor caterer	☐
Marquee size(s) considered and organised (inc. cover for some suppliers)	☐
Considered wet weather contingency	☐
Considered Wet Weather insurance cover	☐
Considered table and seating hire and arranged accordingly	☐
Parasols for shade organised	☐
Central arena created and organised	☐
Bunting sourced	☐
Site drawing plotted	☐
PA system organised	☐
Checked for any caveats with insurers	☐
Arranged a first aid tent and medic/first aid cover or St John's Ambulance	☐
Purchased prizes	☐
Arranged portable toilets	☐

CHAPTER 13

Complete Itinerary

LINKS DEARNEY COMMUNICATIONS

It's going to be a

'spectacular, spectacular' celebration!

FINAL ON SITE ITINERARY

Private & Confidential

June's copy

If this document is found unattended, please return to hotel reception. Thank you

---

Misc.

H&S adviser (James Newitt) has forwarded copies of the location's a) fire risk assessment, b) H&S risk assessment for associated event and c) general H&S policy of their location. Documents retained on file. James has checked all details.

All guests have been sent full directions to the location (inc. transport links) and informed that there is plenty of complimentary car parking available.

Authorised signatures have been confirmed as June Weatherer and Lilly Smart.

No disabled guests are attending.

No particular dress code applies to corporate guests.

Friday 24th July:

07.00   June collects van from office (3 day hire - £95.25 plus VAT. On account) and loads with:

      Box 1:   CDs (inc. Moulin Rouge soundtrack)
              Directional signage
              6 x radios, holsters, coverts, spare batteries and battery charger
              Petty cash and tip (£100)
              Place cards (in table order)
              Table names (created in house)
              Table plans (2 x types – alphabetical and floor – created in house)
              Themed menus (created in house)
              6 x itineraries
              Memory stick (inc. all key documents)
              Lap top
              ID badges

      Box 2:   Prizes for casino
              Swags and flags

      Box 3:   Tool box

      Box 4:   Recycle bin

07.30   June departs office and drives to location.

08.00   Main function room (The Palace Suite) access available for set up.
(Discounted to £1,800.00 inc VAT – all hotel costs are quoted inclusive of VAT ie £1,531.92 plus VAT.) Minimum capacity to safeguard the main function room is 150 guests.

Access available into Production Office.

Air conditioning is featured in the Palace Suite. (Natural daylight and large opening windows also in situ.)

WIFI is not available. An outside line and Broadband has been arranged in the Production Office. Good mobile coverage throughout the hotel.

Outside line and internet facility provided free of charge. Usage will be charged for accordingly.

Business facilities are available in the Business Lounge.
Faxing is £1.00 per copy for UK and £2.00 per page for O'seas. Photocopying is £0.15 per copy for B&W and £0.30 per copy for Colour. Printing is £0.10 per A4 sheet. All costs are inc VAT.

08.30   June arrives at hotel and unloads in loading bay 1.

Hotel have been provided with all details of vehicles and times when deliveries or unloading expected.

Trolleys are available from the porter's cabin. Porter assigned to help unload boxes and transfer to the Production Office. When boxes unloaded, June to move vehicle and place in parking space.

When in Production Office, June to check on furniture and arrange any additional chairs or tables. To set up laptop. Check on pre arranged outside line and internet facility. Also to check that the 4 x table plan holders (which take up to A3 size documents) and 5 x directional holders (which take up to A4 size documents) have been placed in Production Office.

Coffee and Danish pastry arranged. (£3.50 inc VAT. £2.98 plus VAT.)

09.30   Meeting with conference & banqueting team – take itinerary and spare radio to give to the acting point of contact throughout the event.

Meeting with Kim Sweets, Banqueting Manager.

To discuss:

- our understanding of event (go through hotel's function sheet and itinerary)
- establish banqueting manager(s) for duration
- drink allocation process
- rowdy behaviour procedures
- late checkout availability
- dietary process
- communication between event manager(s) and hotel staff
- check that the stage and dance floor is in position ready for production company's arrival and that the DJ's small stage is also in position

Then to embark on a dilapidation tour and to check on Lilly Smart's assigned upgraded room (Change to alternative room if applicable.)

10.00   Fire Alarm testing takes place. (No evacuation needed.)

Lighting, sound and red curtain back drop arrives (Burt Noise and Mark Tuning). £1,680.00 plus VAT. Unloads in loading bay 1 - leaves vehicle in loading bay. Commences set up.

Loading bays are situated with a direct load into the Palace Suite.

June to meet to check all is OK when meeting with hotel concludes.

10.30   Arrival of Event Managers (Issie Bright, Sophie Smiley and Louise Glee). All have own insurance cover.

June to phone Event Managers if not arrived on time. (List of mobile numbers featured on Contact sheet.)

Car share. Issie is driving and passengers are Sophie and Louise. To park vehicle in car park.

All Event Managers are wearing casual but smart clothes and trainers for set up and have brought with them black trousers, black T shirt and black shoes for the evening.

All to check in.

Arrival of H&S manager (James). James is arriving by train/taxi and walking short distance to hotel.

10.45 All to gather in the Production Office to meet June. Tea, Coffee and biscuits plus a bowl of fruit, including bananas, and 2 x large jugs of still water arranged for this time. (For five.)

2 x servings of refreshments also provided for Burt and Mark in Palace Suite. £43.00 inc VAT. £36.59 plus VAT.

James to sort and distribute radios. (Label all radios – June, Issie, Sophie, Louise and James (hotel has its radio already) - sort out coverts and select channel 1 – spare batteries placed on charge.) June to provide Issie, Sophie, Louise and James with a copy of the itinerary, highlighter pen and their ID badge.

11.00 Production meeting to be held by June for event managers and James. (Itineraries, highlighter pens and radios needed.)

Walk through all areas being utilised and test radios.

Back in the Production office. Event Managers to then identify their own specific duties.

James to hold H&S meeting with Kim and their designated H&S officer, Mark Cross, and then to undertake the Dynamic Risk Assessment.

Max capacity for the main function room is 300 x guests in total. (Floor plan obtained based on maximum and 200 x guests.)

11.45 James to brief the Event Management team on H&S aspects.

12.00 Issie to check that the hotel have laid out 25 x 5' round tables – allowing for 8 x guests per table. (No top table required.)

Sophie to check on the welcoming board to read…*Links Dearney Communications – Evening Celebration*.

Louise to place directional signs into holders and place table plans into table plan holders.

2 x Table plan styles to be utilised. (Style 1: 1 x A4 sheet with Alphabetical list stating name of guests followed by their table description. Style 2: 1 x A4 sheet floor plan indicating table layout.)

Hotel has been provided with Style 2 which also highlights the guests that are vegetarian and/or require any special dietary needs. (12 x vegetarian. 2 x no dairy.)

June to check with Kim that all is on schedule for lunch. To check layout of River View Suite. £150.00 inc VAT. £127.66 plus VAT room hire charged. (Also being utilised as supplier's changing room and subsistence room. 2 x partition doors enable private dressing. One for male and one for female. Mirror, rail and hangers placed in both of these sections.)

In the other section of the River View Suite, tables and chairs for 17 x personnel have been arranged.

James to continue undertaking H&S duties.

12.30 Lunch is served for 7 in the River View suite.

Lasagne, green salad, coleslaw, 3 bean salad and cold meats.
Wholemeal rolls and butter. (Chips have also been requested by the crew.)
2 x jugs of orange juice, 1 x jug of still and 1 x bottle of sparkling water.
Tea and Coffee (£14.00 per person x 7 = £98.00 inc VAT – special crew rate and £51.00 inc VAT for drinks) £126.81 plus VAT.

13.30 Event Management team to prepare for theming and set up.

Sound, backdrop and party lighting all complete.

June to discuss location of hand held radio microphone.

(Burt and Mark to depart – Mark the sound engineer to return at 18.00.)

14.00 Hotel has authorised that public areas can be set up from this time.

Sophie and Louise to place directional signage. James to check.

Issie to take the Tool Box and commence erecting the swags and flags in the Moat Suite (pre dinner drinks area). £118.00 plus VAT for theming. Moat Suite is provided free of charge.

Hotel setting up 8 x 3ft occasional tables in this area (with cloths). Flags to be placed on to tables.

When Sophie and Louise have completed erecting the directional signage, to join Issie to help.

(All theming has been confirmed as being fireproofed and adheres to H&S requirements.)

Hotel laying out tables with crockery, napery and glasswear. Also to provide table name 'holders' June to generally 'float' and liaise with hotel as and when needed.

15.00   Balloons arrive. (Cheryl Ribbon). All balloons arriving inflated. Van unloads at loading bay 1 and are all to be brought into the Moat Suite. Cheryl to then move van to parking space. June to greet.

120 x helium balloons – 20 x bunches of 6 balloons. £156.00 plus VAT Cheryl to create bunches and June to place in situ. (No restriction on helium balloons in Moat Suite.)

James to monitor.

16.00   Florist arrives. (Maria Rose) To unload in loading bay 1 and leave vehicle in situ.

June to greet.

Maria to set up themed table arrangements. 25 table centres @ £55.00 = £1,375.00 plus VAT.

Issie to place table plans (one set in Moat Suite and one set in Palace Suite) and then layout place cards on the tables, menu cards and table names into holders.

Sophie to call the DJ and check that he is on schedule to arrive at 18.00.

Sophie and Louise to commence erecting red and gold swags in the Palace Suite.   Red and gold swags £158.00 plus VAT.

Cheryl to move other balloons into the Palace Suite, June to direct where to place accordingly. 220 x floor mounted balloons @ £330.00 plus VAT (22 x bunches of 10 balloons.)

June to tie 3 x heart shaped balloons to each table centre. 75 x red heart balloons @ £112.50 plus VAT.

1 x flask of tea, 1 x flask of coffee, biscuits and 1 x jug of orange juice served in the Palace Suite for 7. £41.50 inc VAT. £35.32 plus VAT.

17.30   Lilly Smart arrives. Lilly arriving by taxi.

Lilly checks in, takes her luggage to her room and then joins the team in the Palace Suite.

June to meet and show Lilly around.
James to hand to Lilly the H&S notes that she will be giving at the start of the meal and discuss.

Cheryl and Maria to depart.

Band arrives – parks vehicle in loading bay 1 and unloads into Palace Suite. (£1,300.00 plus VAT inc own PA). Main contact is Bryan Note. See band details featured on Contact sheet.

Band are to set up on the main stage.

Sophie and Louise to get changed. (Collect T shirts from Production Office.)

Place radios on charge whilst changing.

Replenishment of coffee flask and tea £60.00 inc VAT . £51.06 plus VAT.

James to monitor.

18.00   Sound engineer returns (Mark) to be on hand…

DJ (Steve Smooth) arrives and parks vehicle in loading bay 2 and unloads into Palace Suite. £700.00 plus VAT. After unloaded to move vehicle to parking space. See DJ details featured on Contact sheet.

DJ featured on smaller stage, stage left.

Sophie and Louise to return and pick up their radios whilst June and Issie to go and get changed. (June and Issie's radios placed on charge.) James also to leave and get changed after placing radio on charge.

Sophie to establish e.t.a. if Band or DJ fail to arrive as scheduled.

Louise to monitor arrival and sound checks.

18.30   DJ to undertake sound check. (Utilising sound system erected by production company.)

June and Issie to return and pick up their radios.

James to continue to monitor.

Accordionist and Violinist arrive, to unload and place car in car park. £395.00 plus VAT (Russ Button and Simon Strummer.) Issie to greet and show them to the River View Suite (changing area). Details as per Contact sheet.

Soft drinks of water and orange juice with plenty of glasses placed into the River View Suite. Issie to chase if not present. Sandwiches also arranged for Russ and Simon (£58.40 inc VAT) £49.70 plus VAT.

18.45   Band sound check.

June to check that the Moat Suite is all ready for pre dinner drinks and to undertake last minute checks (inc directional signs are in the right place and have not been moved).

Louise and Sophie to continue to monitor the Palace Suite.

Casino arrives. Suzi Deck is main contact. Parks in loading bay 2 and unloads. Vehicle remains. 5 x tables (1 x Roulette, 1 x Craps, 2 x Black Jack and 1 x Poker - £1,375.00 plus VAT inc costumes.) Paul Heart also arrives to help set up. 3 x additional croupiers to arrive later. Details as per Contact sheet. Louise to direct accordingly.

Can Can girls arrive. Dawn Diamond is main contact. 6 x Can Can dancers inc costumes - £1,560.00 plus VAT. (Dancers are: Delilah, Jacquie, Claire, Kay, Justine and Phillipa.) Details as per Contact sheet. Sophie to collect CD from Dawn plus the themed CDs and general CDs from the Production Office and give to Mark the sound engineer for checking. Sophie then to direct girls to the River View Suite to drop off costumes – Issie to meet. Any vehicles to be left in car park after unloading.

19.00   Issie to direct girls back to Palace Suite. Can Can girls to rehearse - not in costume.

MC arrives (Philip Host). Issie to greet and show to the River View Suite. MC and costume. (£600.00 and £60.00 plus VAT.)

June to ensure that 2 x cloakroom staff in position. £10.00 inc VAT. £8.51 plus VAT per hour – 5 hours booked. No tipping required. Enough storage for 350 coats.

19.15   Rehearsals cease. Dancers led back into the River View Suite by Sophie.
Louise to check that the Casino people are happy and then after last minute checks of the

Palace Suite, returns to Production Office.

Accordionist and Violinist in position in the Moat Suite ready for early arrivals.

All Event Managers and H&S manager in situ. (Louise at main door to greet, Issie by the cloakroom, Sophie on route to the Moat Suite and June in the Moat Suite. James to be with main body of guests throughout the evening, monitoring.)

Photographer arrives and is a staff member from the graphics department - Daniel Flash. Daniel has been forwarded an Itinerary. (Lilly has provided Daniel with a call sheet of all the photograph shots she would like. Précis version, 'reportage' style throughout the evening, no formal shots.) Daniel to wear DJ for the evening.

19.30   Guests arrive (198 expected)

All guests arriving under their own steam. (Ample car parking – free of charge. Local tube and mainline station are 5 and 10 mins walking distance respectively.)

Guests wishing to take a comfort break can utilise the toilets close to the cloakroom. (Closest toilets for the Palace Suite are along the corridor – directional signs already set up.)

Smoking is allowed outside on the terrace. (Weather cover provided.)

Tray service:

Glass of house champagne is from £6.00 inc VAT (£5.11 plus VAT).
Glass of house wine is from £4.95 inc VAT (£4.21 plus VAT).
Soft drinks are: £1.90 inc VAT (£1.61 plus VAT).

Allowed a total budget of approx. £2,315.00 inc VAT (£1,970.00 plus VAT).
Anticipate 2 x glasses of champagne, 20 x glasses of wine, 50 x servings of soft drinks.

Hotel will inform June should 90% of this allocation be reached so that June can seek approval from Lilly to serve additional drinks in excess of budget.

Food is served in the River View Suite for 4 x band, 1 x sound eng, 1 x DJ, 2 x casino, 7 x Can Can, 1 x MC and 1 x caricaturist. Total of 17. (Caricaturist arriving a little later.)

Diet coke, regular coke, 4 x jugs of orange juice, tap and sparkling water.

17 x £16.00 = £272.00 inc VAT and drinks are £59.10 inc VAT. £281.78 plus VAT.

3 x vegetarians, namely: Philip, Claire and Suzi

Shepherds Pie
Vegetable Pasta
Cold Meats (Ham & Chicken)
Salads (Green, Coleslaw, Waldorf)
Brown and White rolls and butter

19.45   Canapés are distributed from two serving points.

Canapés are £4.00 inc VAT (£3.40 plus VAT).

Mini potato pancake with a seared rare roast beef
and mustard cream (hot)
Smoked and fresh salmon tartare with peppercorns
on toasted brioche (cold)

Caricaturist arrives (Jack Draw) and goes directly to the River View Suite. Jack to phone Issie when he arrives. Details are as per the Contact sheet. Issie to chase if he has not arrived as scheduled. (£350.00 plus VAT plus £34.00 allowance for costume). Jack to eat with other suppliers upon arrival.

Suzi and Paul to go to the River View Suite to have dinner when finished setting up.

All entertainers (apart from 3 croupiers) now on site. (All Risk Assessments and copies of Insurance have been sent by James to Lilly for files.) Although no suppliers have a Business Continuity Plan in place, as they have been secured through an agency, the agency has a BCP in place. Agent has been informed that it is not acceptable for suppliers to hand out any promotional literature.

20.00   When most guests have arrived, Louise, Issie and Sophie to join June in Moat Suite.

20.15   June and Sophie to check that the hotel staff are all up to speed. Also to check on the level of lighting, that candles are lit and background music (Themed CD) is playing. In addition, to judge if the temperature is cool enough with natural ventilation or whether the air conditioning needs to be activated. (To monitor throughout the event.)

Issie to place MC on stand by.

Event Management to line the route. Louise and Issie ready to start moving guests through, Sophie to line route to Palace Suite and June waiting in Palace Suite.

20.20   MC to make an announcement and lead the guests through into dinner. (The Palace Suite.)

20.30   All guests to have taken their seats. All Event Management staff in the Palace Suite on hand to direct guests to their appropriate tables.

June to hand Lilly the hands free microphone for Lilly to welcome guests and to read the general H&S announcement. (Mark to turn down the music and manage the level of the microphone.)

20.35   Dinner is served.

James to constantly monitor the situation – mindful of naked flames on each table setting.

The hotel is providing its French chef for this function (even though the menu is not traditional French fayre).

Menu is £39.00 inc VAT (£33.19 plus VAT). (Produce has been sourced locally where feasible and menu utilises produce in season.)

Gothic Tower
Timbale of Prawns, Avocado and Papaya

(For those who do not like fish the dish can be provided without the Prawns)

Duke's Delight
Supreme of Chicken on a bed of Gourmet Mushrooms and Shallots
Served with an apple laced rosti and fresh garden vegetables

Sautéed giant field Mushrooms marinated in Rosemary and Thyme
Served as above (v)

L'Amour, L'Amour
Banoffee Pie

Ropiteau L'Emage Sauvignon blanc
Ropiteau L'Emage Cabernet Sauvignon

Still/tap and Sparkling Mineral water

Wine is £13.95 inc VAT per bottle (£11.87 plus VAT).

Allocated ½ bottle per person – total budget £1,187.00 plus VAT. (Hotel to inform June when 90% of this allocation has been consumed. June to obtain Lilly's authority to continue serving wine after the limit is exceeded.)
Both wine and water will be served throughout the dining service. (No liqueurs to be offered.)

Jack to be collected from the River View Room by Issie ready to enter the Palace Suite.

20.45   Jack to perform at tables (caricaturist).

20.50   When all guests are seated and are being served their starter – event management to go to the ante room alongside the Palace Suite to eat. (Taken in shifts to keep a presence in the main dining area.)

Photographer to join the team as and when ready.

Same menu (2 course - main and dessert) served for special price of £25.00 inc VAT. £21.27 plus VAT. June, Issie, Sophie, Louise and James plus Daniel. 6 @ £25.00 = £150.00 inc VAT. Soft drinks of water, coke and orange juice also served @ £65.60 inc VAT. £183.49 plus VAT.

No special dietary needs or vegetarians.

Louise to check on the entertainers during the course of the dinner.

21.15   3 x Croupiers arrive (Nick, Eric and Lucy). These croupiers do not require subsistence as they have already eaten.

21.45   Team to generally monitor the menu service with Kim the Banqueting Manager.

Issie to collect Can Can girls, Sophie to place Mark, the sound engineer, on stand by. June and Louise on hand in the Palace Suite.

James to continue to monitor.

Jack finishes and departs. June to thank.

22.00   MC to welcome the guests to the 'show'! To announce that the cash bar is now open.

Can Can Dancers perform (with audience participation).

Louise to collect band and wait in the wings. Louise also to collect croupiers.

22.20   MC thanks the Can Can dancers, informs that the casino is now open and welcomes the band onto the stage.

Louise and Sophie to go to Moat Suite and collect balloons – place these on route guests will take when they leave the Palace Suite.

June to thank the Can Can dancers prior to their departure.

Issie to start striking the swags and flags in the Moat Suite and place into the Production Office.

23.00   MC thanks the band and welcomes the DJ.

Band has been informed they can strike their equipment if discreetly undertaken – any major dismantling to be left after the guests have departed.

June to thank the band.

23.30   Casino closes – winnings totted up.

Sophie to collect casino prizes and hand to Lilly.

23.50   DJ announces the winners (3rd, 2nd and 1st) and to retrieve prizes from Lilly.

Last dance/record.

Croupiers start to clear their tables. (To dispose of any fun money into the recycle box in the production office.)

23.55   Event management team to take their places. (June and Sophie directing guests towards cloakroom, Issie by cloakroom and Louise by front door. James where he deems best.)

Taxi rank number is on the Contacts sheet although the hotel porters will call taxis as and when required.

June and Sophie to encourage guests to take the balloons and table arrangements as they leave. (Table arrangements do not incorporate any hired aspects.)

00.00   MC to inform guests the *show* is over….

Event ceases – guests depart.

When the last guest has left the dining room, June and Sophie to start striking any remaining table arrangements and swags.

June to thank MC, Mark and Burt, DJ and Croupiers.

Band strikes any remaining equipment.

Mark is joined by Burt who starts to strike lights, sound and backdrop.

DJ starts to clear away and collects his vehicle and parks behind the band or the casino to load. *All suppliers have confirmed that they wish to depart after the event and do not require overnight accommodation.*

When all guests have departed. Issie and Louise to collect all radios, gather any items that can be recycled and to place into the applicable recycle bins, then to clear the Production Office. Location will dispose of any additional rubbish that is placed by the production office door. Any sensitive documentation along with June's recycle bin to be placed back into the van.

02.00   Event team to have a well earned drink!

03.00   Palace Suite and Production office needs to be clear.

Accommodation:

10 x single occupancy rooms (booked). B&B rate of £150.00 inc VAT per person (£127.66 plus VAT). See Rooming List in pecking order.

Complimentary upgrade arranged for Lilly Smart.

All guests to take their own luggage to their rooms and also to settle any room extras upon departure. (Guests and Event Managers informed of this.)

Mini bars are fully stocked. Complimentary newspapers are provided.

1 x single occupancy and 2 x Twin rooms (Special rate of £160.00 inc VAT per room ie £136.17 plus VAT for twin.)

June Weatherer & Sophie Smiley
Issie Bright and Louise Glee
James Newitt

Special rate of £150.00 inc VAT per person also secured for all those guests arranging their accommodation directly with the hotel. They will have quoted Links Dearney upon booking.

Saturday 25th July:

10.00   June to have a meeting with the Banqueting Manager (or general manager) to briefly discuss the event and to provide a tip for the hotel team to thank them.

Also enclosed at back of itinerary, would be:

- Alphabetical table plan
- Floor plan (indicating where special dietary need guests are seated)
- Contact list of all suppliers (including mobile numbers)
- Rooming list for 10 rooms
- Blank lined paper

CHAPTER 14

Complete Benchmark Schedule

Happiness is a Ticked Off List!

Helpful Contact Details

Helpful Contact Details

Below, is a list of publications, associations and general helpful sites which you may like to refer to, or contact, when planning an event. There are many other associations that you may also like to consider and these can be readily sourced on the internet.

It could be argued that many good companies or individuals choose not to join an association. However, when in a situation where you quite literally don't know where to begin, establishing a supplier bound by an association's code of practice is as good a place to start as any.

Publishers

Conference Blue and Green Book
CMP Information
www.venuefinder.com

Johansens
Conde Nast
www.johansens.co.uk

CES
Hollis Publishing Ltd
www.eventservicesonline.co.uk

Event
Haymarket
www.haymarketgroup.co.uk

M&it (Meetings and Incentive Travel)
Conference and Travel Publications Ltd
www.meetpie.com

Exhibitions

CONFEX
www.international-confex.com

Event UK (previously National Venue Show)
www.event-uk.com

RSVP
www.rsvpevent.co.uk

Associations

Association of Event Venues (AEV)
Represents the interests of venues within the wider events industry.
119 High Street
Berkhamsted
Hertfordshire HP4 2DJ
www.aev.org.uk

Eventia
Represents corporate event organisations and suppliers.
1 Queen Anne's Gate
London SW1H 9TB
www.eventia.org.uk

Design Business Association (DBA)
The Design Business Association exists to promote professional excellence through productive partnerships between commerce and the design industry.
35–39 Old Street
London EC1V 9HX
www.dba.org.uk

Independent Print Industry Association (IPIA)
The Independent Print Industries Association (IPIA) is a non-profit trade association that is dedicated to promoting the highest standards within the Independent Sector of the UK Printing Industry.
Brooklyn House, 44 Brook St,
Shepshed, Leicestershire LE12 9RG
www.ipia.org.uk

The Agents' Association

The Agents' Association (Great Britain) represents and enhances the interests of entertainment agents in the United Kingdom who are willing to be bound by a strict code of conduct and professional ethics. Members' business activities include Agents who handle performing artistes in the pop and rock music industry, television, film, radio, recording, theatre, musicals, cabaret, clubs, cruising and corporate and outdoor events.

54 Keyes House
Dolphin Square
London SW1V 3NA

www.agents-uk.com

Association of British Insurers (ABI)

The ABI represents the collective interests of the UK's insurance industry.

51 Gresham Street
London EC2V 7HQ

www.abi.org.uk

The Association for Conference & Events (ACE)

An information centre and forum for members involved in the creating, marketing, organising, accommodating and servicing of events.

Riverside House
High Street
Huntingdon
Cambridgeshire PE18 6SG

www.martex.co.uk

Association of Event Organisers (AEO)

Providing assistance to all organisations and individuals involved in events and exhibitions; whether organising, exhibiting or visiting an event.

119 High Street
Berkhamsted
Hertfordshire HP4 2DJ

www.aeo.org.uk

Meetings Industry Association (MIA)

A trade association for all organisations involved in the meetings industry (locations and suppliers).

PO Box 515
Kelmarsh
Northamptonshire NN6 9XW

www.mia-uk.org

Institution of Occupational Safety and Health (IOSH)

IOSH is Europe's leading body for health and safety professionals.

The Grange

Highfield Drive

Wigston

Leicestershire LE18 1NN

www.iosh.org.uk

British Florist Association

The only trade association in the florist industry that is recognised by Government both here and in Brussels. The BFA is recognised as the 'voice of the industry' representing nearly 6,500 florists.

68 First Avenue

Mortlake

London SW14 8SR

www.britishfloristassociation.org

The Balloon Association (NABAS)

An Association for both the public and the industry – encouraging standards of good practice within the industry.

Katepwa House

Ashfield Park Avenue

Ross-on-Wye

Herefordshire HR9 5AX

www.nabas.co.uk

National Association of Disk Jockeys (NADJ)

An association to promote and represent disk jockeys who comply with the highest possible standards of professional conduct.

12 Leasowe Road

Wallasey

Kerseyside CH44 2BX

www.nadj.org.uk

Professional Lighting & Sound Association (PLASA)

A trade association representing companies who manufacture, supply, hire, install or use lighting, sound, audio-visual and related technologies within the events industry.

Redoubt House

1 Edward Road

Eastbourne BN23 8AS

www.plasa.org

The Photographers Association (AOP)

The AOP brings professional photographers together, protecting their rights and promoting photography.

81 Leonard Street

London EC2A 4QS

www.the-aop.org

Association of Translation Companies (ATC)

Dedicated to not only representing the interests of translation companies, but also to serving the needs of translation purchasers.

5th Floor

Greener House

66-68 Haymarket

London SW17 4RF

www.atc.org.uk

British Security Industry Association (BSIA)

The British Security Industry Association is the trade association for the professional security industry in the UK.

Kirkham House

John Comyn Drive

Worcester WR3 7NS

www.bsia.co.uk

Adventure Activity Licensing Authority (AALA)

The Adventure Activities Licensing Scheme is a joint venture between the Adventure Activities Licensing Authority (a role designated to the Health and Safety Executive on 1st April 2007) and the Adventure Activities Licensing Service, which is under contract with the Health and Safety Executive to operate the scheme on their behalf. The scheme ensures that those who provide certain adventure activities will have their safety management systems inspected and where appropriate, a licence issued.

44 Lambourne Crescent

Cardiff Business Park

Llanishen

Cardiff CF14 5GG

www.aala.org

Association of Mountaineering Instructors (AMI)

The Association of Mountaineering Instructors is the representative body for professionally qualified Mountaineering Instructors in the British Isles. AMI is committed to promoting good practice in all mountaineering instruction.

Siabod Cottage

Capel Curig

Conwy LL24 0ET

www.ami.org.uk

The British Canoe Union (BCU)

The BCU is the lead body for canoeing and kayaking in the UK.

18 Market Place

Bingham

Nottingham NG13 8AP

www.bcu.org.uk

Royal Yachting Association (RYA)

The RYA is the UK's national association for all forms of recreational and competitive boating, representing sailing, motorcruising, sports boats, windsurfing, inland boating, powerboat racing and personal watercraft.

RYA House

Ensign Way

Hamble

Southampton

Hampshire SO31 4YA

www.rya.org.uk

Nationwide Caterers Association (NCASS)

Independent body in the Mobile Catering industry in the UK. The Association represents mobile caterers, buffet and corporate hospitality caterers and almost anyone in the fast food industry together with Suppliers to the trade.

Association House

89 Mappleborough Road

Shirley

Solihull B90 1AG

www.ncass.org.uk

St John Ambulance

Their mission is to provide an effective and efficient charitable first aid service to local communities.

27 St John's Lane

London EC1M 4BU

www.sja.org.uk

The Performance Textiles Association (Pertexa)

Pertexa represents all facets of the textile industry, from textile production, through conversion, manufacture and on to use. Members include special interest groups for coating, manufacture, marquee hire, inflatable play, healthcare products, load restraint as well as specialist suppliers to the industry.

42 Heath Street

Tamworth, Staffordshire

B79 7JH

www.performancetextiles.org.uk

Association of British Travel Agents (A.B.T.A)

Represents UK travel agents and tour operators.

68–71 Newman Street,

LondonW1T 3AH

www.abta.com

Advice and Guidance

The Law Society

The Law Society is the representative body for solicitors in England and Wales.

www.lawsociety.org.uk

British Standards (BSI)

BSI British Standards is the UK's national standards organisation, recognized globally for its independence, integrity and innovation in the production of standards and information products that promote and share best practice.

BS 8901 is the Specification for a sustainable event management system with guidance for use.

www.bsi-global.com/BS8901

The Health & Safety Commission (HSC)

The Commission is responsible for health and safety regulation in GB. The Health and Safety Executive and local government are the enforcing authorities who work in support of the Commission.

www.hse.gov.uk

Hiscox

Hiscox is a leader in specialist insurance. They seek to provide the best protection and peace of mind for their clients through high quality insurance products, backed with excellent service.

www.hiscox.co.uk

Directgov

Directgov brings together a wide range of public service information and services online. The site also provides access to government directories as well as links to relevant third parties who can offer additional trusted advice and support.

www.direct.gov.uk

Karen Lindsey Consultancy

Training and bespoke corporate event consultancy (design, organisation and management).

www.happinessisatickedofflist.com

www.KLC-UK.com

Acknowledgments

They say that there is a book inside everyone and well, I guess I am proof of that!

Happiness… would not have come into being without the encouragement and support of many people who have been instrumental in my life.

Firstly, to my family who have been the most supportive family anyone could ever wish for and who helped to instil the work ethic that I hold true to this day.

I have been very fortunate to have worked together with my mother (Dawn), my father (Jeff) and my brother (Mark). Dawn, a renowned florist, created some absolutely fabulous designs and her floral décor, is still commented upon to this day. My father was always working tirelessly in the background and could regularly be spotted de-thorning hundreds of roses to help in the preparation as well as offering much needed massages to the feet and shoulders of the weary event team. Mark later joined the company in the capacity of sales and marketing and was a hit with the clients and employees alike – happy days!

My thanks must also extend, way back, to Dan Silver who taught me the true meaning of attention to detail and accuracy and introduced to me the concept of an 'itinerary' whilst Caroline Adair gave me the opportunity to join her company and follow in her footsteps as a proficient event organiser.

Organising is one thing but having the privilege of organising events for some fabulous clients is another. My 'bestest' and most long standing clients include Simon Lee and Peter Dutton who have supported me in my quest for over a decade and who were, indeed, instrumental in coaxing me to actually put pen to paper. I have been fortunate to develop a number of close relationships including Becky, Derek and Leigh from KFC, Jo, Darren, Sue and Lisa from Universal Pictures and, Natasha and Nadia from Momentum Pictures. In later days, John Runyard made his mark and I, too, enjoyed 'ticking off the list' for his very special event. I truly thank them all for their support and encouragement.

Prior to becoming a consultant, I formed a company with my partner, Ronnie Dunnett, and it has to be said that without his very special people skills and *broker* attitude, Leaps & Bounds would not have had such an ultimate kick start in life. His colleagues and my long term friends 'Burt' Reynolds and 'Bungy' Williams helped us out considerably in the early days, for which I will be eternally grateful. Many years later… Darcy Willson-Rymer and I joined forces - I learned a great deal from Darcy and came to view him as my mentor and much appreciated his valuable input and guidance.

I have been extremely fortunate to work alongside some exceptional people who showed so much dedication. One in particular was Phillipa Burnett who was initially employed as my PA but progressed into becoming one of the most conscientious senior event organisers that I have ever had the pleasure of working with. Heartfelt thanks must also be extended to Jacquie Browne, Claire Norris and Delilah Sullivan along with 'Josh' Jordan who have all worked way beyond the call of duty on many an occasion.

I talk in my book about the importance of securing and developing long term relationships and those people who still hold a special place in my heart for supplying the best services and also pulling out all the stops, has to include Nick Sprake, Tom Button and Matt King who helped me to consistently provide first class events. John Foster always kept me on the straight and narrow and still does to this day, thank you, John.

Although I took to writing this book like a *duck taking to water*, many people have also checked through various chapters and their contribution has been truly much appreciated. These include: 'Josh', Nick Sprake, Mark Ridout, Pippa King, Roan Fair, Neil Vaughan and Tania Riddiford. I also asked some friends and family to proof read the entire book to provide much needed feedback and so many thanks must also go to Steve Mills, Delilah, Mum and especially Eric, my stepfather, who assiduously checked my gramma!

My final thanks must go to Simon Meads who has always been my *rock* and soul mate, Stroma who has been like a daughter to me and my lovely husband, Bryan, whose constant support never ceases to amaze me. I simply couldn't have performed in the capacity as MD of an event company, taken the *bull by the horns* and followed my dream of becoming a corporate event consultant and trainer whilst at the same time penning this book, without his stoic support. Bryan, words can never express how much your support and love means to me.

Thank you all…

General Index

A-Z Guide 159-165
ABTA/IATA 153
Accident log 98, 134
Accommodation 26, 27, 29, 81, 101, 125
Activity days 134-136
    Considerations 135, 136
    Damage deposit 136
    Fitness levels 135
Administrative housekeeping 17, 18
Advance party 155
Advice and guidance 225
Agents 68, 126
    Representation brochure 68
Air conditioning 27, 64
Alcohol 134, 142, 155, 160
Allergies 60
Allocation contract 149
Associations 12, 143, 220 – 225
Attitude 159, 160-163
Audience participation 64
Authorisation 9, 28, 159
Authorised signatories 151
Autocue 121
Award ceremonies 126, 127
Awards table 126
Awards/trophies 126

Back projection 118
Back up equipment 119
Banqueting table 24, 96
Banqueting team meeting 93-95
Behaviour 94
Benchmark schedule 42-46, 121, 159
Benchmark schedule (complete example) 213-215
Birthday cake 83
Body language 97
Borrowed time 159
Broadband (WIFI/ISDN) 27, 120
BS 8901
(Specification for a sustainable event management system) 17, 18, 82
Business continuity plan 69
Business facilities 26

Carbon footprint 81, 82
Car parking 82
Caterers 72

Ceiling height 119, 120
Celebrity host 126
Changing room 153
Check-in 151, 154
Check-out 155
Coaches 149
Code of conduct 16
Coffee cups 60
Colour coding 39, 46
Commemorative gift 106
Commission 11
Communication 94
Complimentary upgrade 29
Conferences 30, 117-125
    Break out rooms 118
    Location suitability 119
    Presentations 122
    Presentation timings 152
    Projection space and distance 118
    Questions 117, 123, 163
    Speaker and speaker support 117
    Set up 120
    Strap line 122
    Template slide 122
    Timeline 121
    Vision 117
Conference and banqueting 13
    Banqueting manager 93, 94, 159
Conference calls 154
Confetti cannons 152
Confidentiality 80, 161, 164
Confirmation 164
    Location   29
Contingency 22, 69, 72
Contract 89
    Location 29-31
    Supplier 74
Contracting party 30, 110-112
Control position 118
Copyright 51, 58, 123
Corkage charges 63
Corporate packs 27, 28
Costing allocations 23
Costing spreadsheets 20, 27
Creativity 160
Credential checks 68
Credit card 152
Crew rates 81

Dance floor 64

Data protection 102
Dates and deadlines 42, 43
Day delegate rate 16
Debrief document 106
Delegate pack 125
Deliveries 82
Diary date 52
Disabled facilities 151
Document management 18, 19
Dress code 26, 80, 138, 160, 164
Drink allocation 93
Drinks reception 56-58
    Drink 56
    Entertainment 56, 57
    Nibbles 56, 57

Early arrivals 96
Employment status 80
Entertainment 50, 56, 63-67, 141
Establishing the brief 5-7
    Key questions 6, 7
Evacuation 94
Event brief 7-9, 35, 49, 118, 160
Event costing 19-24, 27, 43, 49, 69-71, 77, 83-87,
105, 159
Event finalisation 88, 89
Event manager 79-81, 164
Event manager meeting 95
Event organiser's file 17
Event timings 100
Exclusivity 10, 129
Exhibitions 12, 68, 220
Extra costs sheet 18, 19

Family fun days 141-143
    Age range 141
    Format 142, 143
    Location 141
    PA system 143
    Timings 141
Feedback 101
File management 106
Film and video 50, 51
Fire alarm tests 26
First aid 98, 134, 143
First or second option 16
Floor plan 24, 58, 94
Flowers 83
Food intolerances 155
Fraternizing 154

Front projection 118
Function room usage 30, 80, 81, 102, 129

Gate-crashers 149
Gifts 150
Guest list 43, 89, 125
Guest numbers 124, 151

Hats
    'Creative' 50
    'Environment' 82
    'Event Organiser' 6, 21, 43, 49, 78
    'Guest' 6, 20, 25, 38, 50, 53, 78
Head Sales Office 12
Health & Safety 43, 69, 94, 109-114, 130, 149, 163
    Adviser 112
    Announcement 111, 153
Housekeeping 26, 111
Hydration 96, 160

ID Badges 89
Important documents 19
In-house map 154
'In writing' 13, 28, 74, 164
Insurance 89, 130, 153, 154
    Employer's liability 109
    Professional indemnity 109, 112
    Public liability 69, 80, 109, 112
    Wet weather 142
Internet 12, 50, 68
Invitation 6, 21, 43, 52-55
Invoices 105, 161
Itinerary 35-42, 93, 95, 121, 129, 130, 161, 165
Itinerary (complete example) 195-210

Late check-out 94
Lead-in time 6
Licences 150
Lighting 64
Lists 12, 13, 65, 89
Location brief 13-15, 24, 118
Location, location, location 9-17
Location search 11
Location/venue find agency 11
Logistical process 78-84
    Personnel 78, 79
Logo 153
Luggage 150
Marquees 142, 143
Maximum capacity/numbers 30, 119

Measurements 50, 155
Medical incident 94, 98
Medical questionnaire 133, 135
Memory stick 82, 89
Menu 60, 61
Menu tasting 62
Microphone 156
Minimum numbers 30
Mobile phone 27, 74, 80, 89, 149, 153
Music 57, 60
 Walk on/walk off 127

Naked flame 59

OFSTED 143
Optional extra list 67, 72

Pecking order 29, 155
Personalised covering letter 54, 78
Petty cash 83
Phobias 54
Photographer 65, 127, 139
Place cards 59, 94, 96
Pointer form 111, 153
Power 119
Press and product launches 137-140
 Design 137, 138
 Dress code 138
 Goodybags 140
 Location 137
 Objectives 137
 Press release 138, 139
 Timings 139
Preview 122
Prizes 65, 134, 143
Production brief 118, 119, 123
Production company 118-124, 127
Production meetings 88, 94
Production office 93
Progress meetings 46, 162
Provisional hold 16
PRS Licence 121
Publishers 219

Radios (walkie-talkies) 79, 94, 95
Ratio 79, 130
Recycling 18, 26, 82, 102
References 68
Reference books 50
Refurbishment 149

Registration 125
 Badges 125, 139
 Pre-registration 151
Rehearsals 122, 123
Research 73
Restrictions 16, 120, 135
Rider 84
Risk assessments 69, 95, 109, 110, 130, 142
 Dynamic 95, 110-112
 Fire 110
 Generic 95, 110, 112
Room extras 152
Room hire 17, 24, 120
Rooming lists 88, 89, 153
Room priority 154
RSVP 43, 59
Rubbish 102
Running order 124, 127

Seating 117, 126
Seating configuration 24
Security 149
Security deposit 101
Serving staff 63
Severity x probability table 111
Shifts 100
Show reel 121
Signage 50
Simultaneous events 152
Site visit 25, 26-28, 49, 120, 162
Smoking 152, 162
Special dietary needs 60, 74, 81, 88, 94
Special needs 54
Spreadsheet headings 21, 49
Stage environment 63, 64
Star cloth curtain 64
St John's ambulance 143, 224
Storage boxes 89
Stress 100
Strike 101
Subsistence 81, 82, 84, 124, 125
 Room 81
Suppliers 43, 67-74, 106, 143
 Confirmation 73
 Document 106
 Preferred 68, 150
 Recommendation 68
 Terms and conditions 69, 84, 134, 136
Sustainable event 17, 18, 26, 69, 80-82

Table arrangements 59, 60
Table configuration 24
Table numbers 58
Table plan (s) 58, 59, 89, 94, 127
    Holder 156
Talk back system 124
Team Building 128-133
    Challenge by choice 133
    Company 130-132
    Event brief 128
    Facilitators 130
    Format 131
    Instructors 130, 132
    Kit list 132
    Location style 128, 129
    Objectives 128
    Profiling tools 130
    Questions 128, 163
    Round robin 130
    Score sheets 132
Teaser 51, 52
Terms and conditions
    Location 30, 31, 42, 163
    Supplier 136, 163
Thank you 106
Theme and theming 10, 30, 49-67, 125, 130, 141
    Hired 152
    Theme list 65-67
    Theme names 61, 62
Ticked off list! 19, 101, 106, 161
Time frame 42, 43, 46
Time line 42
Time management 163
Tipping 83, 102
To Do List 18, 19, 161
Toilet facilities 129, 143, 151
Tool box 78, 95, 163, 169, 170
Tourist board 11, 12
Trade books/CD ROM 11, 12, 68
Transfers 155
Translators 125
Transportation 21, 79, 82, 83, 150
Trophies/awards 126
Twenty four hour delegate rate 16, 81

Ultimate tick list 46, 65, 88, 164, 173-191
Unforeseen situations 97-98, 161

VAT 28, 36, 160
Vegetarians 61

Visualisation 20, 21, 25, 26, 78, 79, 82, 123

Walkie-talkies (radios) 79, 94, 95
Weather cover 129, 142
Welcome board 152
Welcome letter 155
Who's who 154
Wine 62, 63, 150, 151
Word of mouth 12, 68
Working in advance 99
WOW factor 59, 160